Business Management and Enterprise

A Resource for Year 12 ATAR

Jason Hinton

Business Management and Enterprise: A resource for Year 12 ATAR
1st Edition
Jason Hinton

Cover design: Leanne Quince, GraphicsAbove

Any URLs contained in this publication were checked for currency during the production process. Note, however, that the publisher cannot vouch for the ongoing currency of URLs.

First published in 2015 by Impact Publishing.
This edition published in 2018 by Cengage Learning Australia.

For product information and technology assistance,
in Australia call **1300 790 853**;
in New Zealand call **0800 449 725**

For permission to use material from this text or product, please email
aust.permissions@cengage.com

ISBN 978 1 92 520707 1

Cengage Learning Australia
Level 7, 80 Dorcas Street
South Melbourne, Victoria Australia 3205

Cengage Learning New Zealand
Unit 4B Rosedale Office Park
331 Rosedale Road, Albany, North Shore 0632, NZ

For learning solutions, visit **cengage.com.au**

Printed in Malaysia by Papercraft
4 5 6 7 8 9 24

Acknowledgements

The author would like to gratefully acknowledge the following people for their feedback on particular sections of the text.

Matthew Sambrailo

Jeff Kane

James Hallifax

Contents

Contents

Introduction

The world is becoming smaller. Technology is bringing nations and communities together and creating business opportunities. Australian businesses can access global markets and international expansion at their fingertips.

But technology is not the only tool. Understanding global diversity and its impact on success is also very important when devising business strategies and building relationships.

As individuals we interact with global businesses every day. It is important to understand global business from the point of view of a consumer, a citizen and a business person.

Themes

The units each have a particular focus.

- **Unit 3:** the focus is on international business growth. How a domestic business can expand into global markets.

- **Unit 4:** the focus is on global business operations and how to manage the challenges of operating globally.

Unit content

The content for each unit of Business Management and Enterprise is split into three main sections. These main sections form the structure of the text and are as follows.

- **Environments:** political and legal, economic, socio-cultural and technological (PEST)
- **Management:** marketing and operations
- **People**

Throughout the book, suggested YouTube searches are given. These videos illustrate and expand on the information provided by the book and can be used when learning about a topic and completing activities.

The unit content outlined in the text is studied in conjunction with a range of relevant activities.

Activities

Activities are found at the end of each chapter and in Examination question chapters and Externally set tasks. They have been split up as follows.

Topic study

These are aimed at checking basic comprehension of the content in the previous chapters. They require the student to be able to define and explain terms and theories.

Business research

These are activities and worksheets available on the internet, or a question that must be researched using web resources. All directly relate to the content of chapters and allow for interactive application of skills and knowledge. These activities include individual tasks and group tasks. Group tasks involve individual work of the group members with a summary presentation completed as a group.

Response

These activities take concepts and strategies from the chapters and apply them to case studies and real world examples. They can be conducted as individual tasks or structured to be group tasks.

Examination questions

These questions are aligned to the examination requirements for the course. These chapters include short answer and extended answer questions. They can be used to prepare for exams and to develop examinations for school based assessment.

A downloadable eBook   +

On the Virtual Study Room

A single integrated learning platform that provides an array of digital learning tools. Students will be able to:

- engage with the latest learning resources in eBook interactive format
- take notes on a dedicated lesson by lesson writing editor
- save these on a personalised MYeP Life (ePortfolio)
- watch videos aligned to content
- engage in virtual quizzes aligned to each chapter
- complete Activities in real time on the interactive writing editor
- undertake additional research with an integrated Google search engine
- chat with other students on Live Chat
- send emails to fellow students and teachers.

 Visit the Impact Publishing website:
www.impactpublishing.com.au
for more details...

UNIT THREE
CHAPTER 1
Global business

**'Globalisation and free trade do spur economic growth,
and they lead to lower prices on many goods.'**
– Robert Reich –

Globalisation is the growing interdependence among nations and encompasses a range of areas such as:

- trade
- investment
- technology
- the flow of capital
- movement of labour.

Evidence of globalisation includes the use of offshore labour, global media, the rise of the English language based Internet, and the spread of consumption of Western fashions in clothes, music and films.

For	Against
• Creates employment and investment in developing countries and increased revenue for governments • Creates a platform and international relationships that can be used to build global standards for fair trade, environmental protection and human rights • Promotes competition which leads to better choices and prices for consumers and businesses • Improves the quality and growth of education and training • Improves the standard of living	• Free trade creates vulnerable countries that do not have protections for local businesses and workers. • Globalisation widens the gap between the rich and the poor where wealthy countries and corporations exploit low pay and conditions. • International companies exploit the lack of environmental protection in some countries. • Globalisation promotes a single culture as the basis for marketing a way of life; encouraging values of materialism and individualism and having an impact on cultural diversity.

ıllıll**VS**ıllıll

Figure 1.1: Reasons for and against globalisation

Globalisation involves the international flow of:

YouTube
Globilisation explained

- **People:** workers, migrants, employees and tourists.

- **Information:** scientific reports, news broadcasts, books, magazines, websites, statistics, marketing research.

- **New technologies:** communication, information, production, distribution, health and transport.

- **Financial resources:** online payment systems, financial deregulation, foreign investment, currency exchange.

- **Culture, images and ideas:** television programs, films, music, artists, entertainers, books and magazines.

- **Goods and services:** imports and exports, tangible, digital.

FACTORS DRIVING GLOBAL BUSINESS

Multinational companies want to increase sales, profits and shareholder value. Globalisation provides that opportunity. As countries cooperate and free trade agreements are signed the barriers to international business are reduced and it is much easier to grow a business into international territories. Governments want to encourage domestic businesses to expand overseas because it results in a flow of profits back into the domestic economy.

Businesses consider global growth because of:

- higher profits and market access in global markets
- reduced technological barriers to movement of goods, services and factors of production
- countries with lower labour and production costs
- extending product life cycles by marketing products in other countries.

The following sections explore other factors that drive global business development.

Financial opportunities and deregulation

In the 1980s, industrialised nations undertook the deregulation of financial markets, reducing barriers to the flow of money between nations and making it easier to attract foreign investment. A vast quantity of money now circulates at the international level in currency deals, stock market transactions and trade. This flow of international capital and ongoing deregulation has produced a financial environment that supports global business.

An increased number of financial transactions and investments in foreign countries has been a result of globalisation. Currency speculation (profit from buying or selling foreign currency) now occurs between countries, businesses and individuals.

Profit margins also encourage globalisation. An Australian wholesaler or retailer may go to a low-cost country to manufacture goods. The opportunity to increase their profit margin and make a business opportunity viable drives global business.

An Australian business may be successful domestically. It may reach market saturation and the maturity stage in the product life cycle. From its domestic success it may have a strong financial position – low debt, high profits and cash reserves. The business can use this strong financial position to go global. There may be markets in other countries for their products and services, licencing opportunities or the possibility of a joint venture. Global business may present a platform to expand a business beyond the domestic markets.

By expanding into overseas markets an Australian business can minimise or hedge against financial losses. The seasons in the southern hemisphere are opposite to the northern hemisphere. A business may have products in Australia that sell well in summer but not winter. The business may be able to counter the sales trough in the Australian winter by selling the products in the northern summer.

Patterns of consumption

Consumers use technology and social networks to easily access and compare products and seek customisation. Smartphone apps and the internet allow customers to research and shop anywhere, anytime. 'Digital' consumers present unique global opportunities for retailers. A business can access customers from around the world. Consumers are more confident and likely to make online purchases.

Businesses use technology to give customers access to avenues such as social media and group purchasing sites to shop, connect with businesses and increase loyalty to brands. Technology has changed the way customers shop, research products and interact with businesses.

Global transportation, secure online payment systems, digital distribution of products and web based shops have also changed the way we buy things. They also provide a strong platform for global business growth.

Consumer behaviour factors that contribute to online global business include:

- access to a greater choice of products
- widespread use of mobile devices
- widespread use of the Internet
- continued strength of the Australian dollar
- increasing level of experience and satisfaction with online shopping amongst consumers across all age groups
- use of social media by both consumers and retailers to drive brand awareness
- secure and reliable payment systems.

Research by Swinburne University found a quarter of Australians are buying online at least once a week, 53% of Australians buy something from the Internet at least once a month and 78% of Australians are regular online shoppers.

Technology and globalisation

Information technology (IT) is a driving factor of globalisation. Improvements in early IT of the 1990s (computer hardware, software, and telecommunications) have caused global improvements in access to information and economic potential. These advances have facilitated efficiency gains in all sectors of the economy. IT provides the communication network that facilitates the expansion of products, ideas and resources among nations and among people regardless of geographic location. Creating efficient and effective channels to exchange information, IT has been the catalyst for global integration.

The internet, email, mobile phones, media and communication networks have all sped up the process of globalisation. They have increased the spread and speed of knowledge transfer and communication. Australian consumers can buy products from any nation in the world, transfer funds between accounts or purchase shares in any major market. Australian businesses can market their products at a fraction of the cost and be exposed to a global marketplace of competition.

Technology also provides opportunities for business,or example business software, manufacturing technologies, medical appliances and processes, communication technologies and mobile apps. These and more are products and services that can be sold around the world.

Globalisation accelerates the change of technology. Technological innovation is encouraged by the potential global markets. Technology is now in the forefront of the modern world creating new jobs, innovations and media sites that are accessed globally. The timeline below shows some of the innovations that have emerged over the last 20 years:

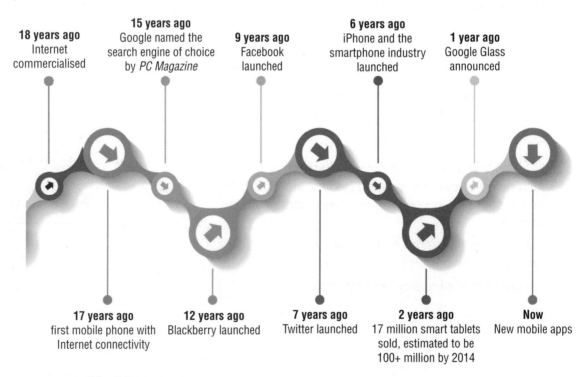

18 years ago
Internet commercialised

15 years ago
Google named the search engine of choice by *PC Magazine*

9 years ago
Facebook launched

6 years ago
iPhone and the smartphone industry launched

1 year ago
Google Glass announced

17 years ago
first mobile phone with Internet connectivity

12 years ago
Blackberry launched

7 years ago
Twitter launched

2 years ago
17 million smart tablets sold, estimated to be 100+ million by 2014

Now
New mobile apps

World Trade Organisation (WTO)

The WTO has growing authority over national governments with restrictions and controls it can impose on nations requiring assistance. Multinational corporations have more economic power than many nations. The WTO sets standards for international trade and for countries participating in Free Trade Agreements. Under WTO rules free trade agreements must:

- eliminate tariffs and other restrictions on all trade in goods between member countries
- eliminate substantially all discrimination against service suppliers from member countries (helping to increase trade in services).

The WTO sets standards for global business including:

- transparency: clear information about policies, rules and regulations
- commitment to lower trade barriers and to increase access to global markets
- centralised databases of trade information
- trade facilitation: the simplification and standardisation of customs procedures, removal of red tape and other measures to simplify trade between countries.

The WTO aims to maintain safe global trade where countries can trade with clear rules, standards and ways to resolve disputes. This should give businesses more confidence and opportunities to increase global trade.

THE IMPACT OF GLOBALISATION

Countries and businesses that are able to take advantage of global trade deregulation have experienced higher levels of economic activity and business opportunity.

Globalisation is also criticised because it is seen as a cause for the loss of national identity, an emerging global monoculture, increasing environmental damage and the exploitation of labour. Free trade agreements are also seen as a means for stronger, wealthier nations to exploit smaller nations.

The impacts of globalisation are explored in this section.

Employment levels

In developing countries there is a lack of capital and government support to grow domestic business and employment. International companies in manufacturing, services, agriculture and mining invest in roads, buildings and technology and create jobs. Developed countries have lost jobs because of the use of labour in the developing world in such things as low-cost manufacturing and services.

Developed countries have also experienced labour shortages because of the movement of highly skilled people (for example in engineering, education, IT and construction) chasing opportunities in the developing world. Government policies on immigration have not kept pace with the global movement of and demand for labour. Labour shortages could be solved if immigration was as free as, and could move with, the flow of capital. Mobility in the labour market is crucial to ensure workers can go where the jobs are as the global economy fluctuates.

The globalisation of labour occurs through international migration but also through the use of technology in outsourcing operations such as call centres and support services.

Offshoring labour or outsourcing business functions to an overseas location is a way to cut costs for business. This may lead to decreased employment locally while employment increases in the overseas country. But the impact of offshoring isn't that simple. Companies only outsource part of their business to emerging low-cost countries. The jobs lost locally are in labour intensive, low skill areas such as manufacturing, for example clothing and electronics. The company cuts costs, and increases profit and productivity, which may allow it to make new investments and expand locally and hire new employees.

Global warming, lack of food security, lack of water security and the disruption of local industries due to climate change and political and financial instability drive international migration and the global movement of labour.

Increased economic activity in developing countries may lead to increased employment as more businesses outsource functions or use offshore labour.

The ethical dilemma about using labour in a country that has lower wages and lower standards for health and safety is discussed in the next chapter.

Spread of skills and technology

Globalisation spreads the knowledge of new inventions, innovations, business models and technology. International companies are investing in, and encouraging governments to support, training and education to build a supply of skilled local workers. Companies can take advantage of people with specialised skills in construction, technology and business, and local language and cultural knowledge.

A company may take their technology, design or process to a low-cost country. By basing manufacturing in another country, local people will be trained and employed. There may also be a transfer of technology because of joint ventures and licencing arrangements.

There has been globalisation in education; Australia has an international education industry generating revenue for the country in the tens of billions of dollars.

It is hoped that the use of information technology may result in rapid development in poor countries. By accessing information, elearning and having an infrastructure that can support business, poor countries may 'leapfrog' stages of economic development and catch up to developed countries. If the quality and access to technology increases it will lead to an increase in a country's competitive advantage which should encourage business and economic growth.

The technology gap between countries is known as the digital divide. The digital divide between countries is the difference between Internet infrastructure, access to the internet and internet speed and stability. This may be an ongoing problem due to an inferior telephone network.

International cooperation

Societies have become richer as they have welcomed people of other cultures. Multicultural societies have diverse lifestyles, music, food, art and ideas. International marketing depends upon understanding the culture and norms of other populations; it increases travel and migration and exposure to diversity.

The growth of globalisation is built on free trade agreements. These are mechanisms for deregulation and creating agreed rules and standards for trade that apply across nations and regions. They involve intergovernmental negotiations and trade agencies working together to reach agreements about improving trade between nations.

Accessing labour, technology, capital and distribution channels in other countries brings businesses together. Australian business people must establish working relationships with business people in other countries. Governments also work together to encourage trade between their nations.

Technology has made global cooperation easier, for example email, videoconferencing, being able to transmit large files and documents easily and securely, and virtual workspaces where people in different locations can work on the same project.

A company in Australia may develop a product based on research by scientists in Europe and manufacture it in Asia.

There are many examples of collaboration between television and film production companies from different countries. Australia has co-production treaties in force with the United Kingdom, Canada, Italy, Ireland, Israel, Germany, Korea, South Africa, Singapore and China and Memoranda of Understanding (MOUs) with France and New Zealand.

Companies working together on official co-productions can take advantage of the financial support provided by their respective governments. Since the start of the co-production support by Screen Australia there have been 158 co-production titles that have been completed or have commenced production.

Co-productions:

- open up new markets for Australian film and television
- enable the sharing of expertise and creativity
- strengthen existing ties and cooperation between countries
- increase the number of high quality films and television programs.

Screen Australia is a federal agency that administers incentives for international co-productions. The Producer Offset provides up to 40% of the budget in financial support from the government. Examples of co-productions include *Happy feet 2*, *Knowing* and *Legends of the guardians: The owls of Ga'hoole*.

Domestic market

Domestic businesses not only compete with each other but also with imported goods. Online shopping and secure online payment systems give consumers access to businesses from around the world.

Globalisation involves the deregulation of international business and free trade agreements between governments of different countries. This makes it easier for businesses from other countries to sell their products in Australia and increases the competition domestic businesses face. To try and compete, domestic businesses may decrease their prices and provide consumers with value which will have an impact on their profits and may lead to some small businesses going out of business.

Global prices and customer demand impact on domestic businesses. If an Australian business exports goods to other countries they will be affected by changes in exchange rates, price and demand overseas. If prices or demand are high the Australian business will earn more income and if prices or demand fall it will reduce their income. This may lead to job losses and cost-cutting by the Australian business to keep operating.

Globalisation also creates opportunities for domestic businesses. They have access to suppliers and products to expand their product line, manage costs and offer customers more choice. A domestic business can offer their products and services to anyone in the world through an online shop. Australian businesses can also access low-cost labour and manufacturing to increase their profit margins.

Tax minimisation

Businesses are entitled to arrange their financial affairs to minimise the tax they have to pay. Tax minimisation is when you legally make arrangements to reduce the amount of tax.

This is different to tax avoidance which is when a business breaks the law to get out of paying the tax they should be paying. This includes investment schemes and legal structures in the form of tax avoidance schemes. A tax scheme moves money through several legal entities, such as trusts and private companies, to avoid or minimise tax. Schemes also involve unethical business reporting so amounts of income can be hidden and payments can be used to claim deductions a business is not entitled to.

Methods businesses use to minimise tax

Two methods businesses use to minimise tax are:

- tax havens
- transfer pricing.

Tax havens

Tax havens are countries with secretive tax and financial systems and low taxes for non-residents and foreign owned companies. It results in less taxes paid to the government where the business is operating. A country can be classified as a tax haven if in terms of taxation and finance there is:

- **a lack of transparency:** no or weak laws about business records and reporting making it difficult to track business transactions, earnings and money
- **a lack of information exchange:** governments and financial institutions do not share information with other governments and resist sharing information to assist international investigations.

Companies benefit by creating a parent company registered in the tax haven country or by creating complex accounting arrangements to transfer global earnings to the tax haven.

The use and establishment of tax havens and transfer pricing arrangements are not necessarily illegal. At the least their use has an ethical aspect that must be considered. Established channels to secrete money and protect it from the inspection of government authorities also creates a system to launder money earned from criminal activities.

Bermuda, Switzerland and the Channel Islands are considered tax havens and have laws designed to attract foreign capital by offering low or no taxes. The local governments benefit from the wealth created by offering financial services to foreign companies.

BUSINESS IN SOCIETY

McDonald's uses royalty payments from franchisees and foreign subsidiaries to route profits to tax havens. The strategies may have allowed it to avoid up to US$1.8 billion in tax in those markets in the years between 2009 and 2013, including €1 billion across Europe and A$497 million in Australia.

BUSINESS IN SOCIETY

Australian company James Hardie[1] tried to avoid their obligation to pay compensation to workers by moving their headquarters to Ireland. American oil company, Exxon, makes profit in the billions but pays no tax in the US because revenue us earned by subsidiaries based in other countries.

YouTube
Tax haven use prompts call for action

1   www.jameshardie.com.au

Transfer pricing

Transfer pricing refers to internal prices and is used by multinational companies to reduce their tax bill. It is when one part of a multinational company sells products or services to another part of the same company in a different country. The prices charged can manipulate profits and the amount of tax they have to pay.

If two unrelated businesses trade with each other at 'arms length', prices are set by the market. The prices charged are similar to what other companies charge each other.

When two businesses that are part of the same multinational company trade with each other, they can artificially distort the price to minimise the overall tax bill.

A company may own a range of businesses. One business sells wood to another business to use to make paper. Both businesses are owned by the same company so the terms of the transaction can be manipulated to avoid tax, tariff and duty payment obligations.

For example, a food business called Global Foods grows crops in Australia, then processes them and sells the finished product in China. Global Foods does this through three subsidiaries; Australia Foods, Bermuda Foods (in a tax haven with zero taxes) and finally China Foods.

> **BUSINESS CONCEPTS**
>
> Accounting firm PwC[2] offers services to help businesses manage their transfer pricing to minimise tax because tax authorities around the world have stricter penalties, new documentation requirements, increased information exchange between government agencies and specialised auditors.

Australia Foods sells the produce to Bermuda Foods at an artificially low price. This means that Australia Foods makes less money and pays less tax in Australia. It could be manipulated on paper for Australia Foods to make a loss and pay no tax. Then Bermuda Foods sells the finished product to China Foods at a very high price. Bermuda Foods makes a big profit because of the low purchase price and high selling price, but pays no tax because they operate in a tax haven. China Foods has artificially low profit because of the high cost of importing the products, so has a low tax bill in China.

Figure 1.2: Transfer pricing

The big profit made in Bermuda does not really exist. It has been created through transfer pricing between parts of the same company. The profit is tax-free and makes the whole company look better on paper than it would otherwise.

---

2   www.pwc.com/gx/en/tax/transfer-pricing/transfer-pricing.jhtml

Australia has tax laws to try and stop this manipulation of transfer pricing by making companies use prices that are reasonable and better reflect what would happen in an arms-length transaction.

YouTube
What is transfer pricing? (by e-Bright)

BUSINESS IN SOCIETY

Bernie Ecclestone owned the lucrative commercial rights for the international sport of Formula One racing. To avoid tax he transferred the rights to a company owned by his wife based in a tax haven. It is estimated that he has avoided paying 40% tax on earnings of over $2 billion.

CHAPTER 2
Home-grown business

'We do not go to work only to earn an income, but to find meaning in our lives. What we do is a large part of what we are.'
– Alan Ryan –

INCENTIVES FOR INTERNATIONAL TRADE

Austrade administers the government's Export Market Development Grants (EMDG) scheme for new and existing international businesses. Financial assistance is in the form of a reimbursement of up to 50% of expenses incurred on eligible export promotion activities. Businesses that have an income of less than $50 million per year and incur at least $15,000 of eligible export expenses are eligible.

Austrade also assists businesses by:

- providing information about international markets and trends
- arranging meetings with potential clients and partners
- providing ongoing support and information.

Austrade provides information and advice to assist Australian companies reduce the time, cost and risk associated with exporting. Austrade also researches overseas markets to look for emerging markets and demand for Australian goods and services.

As well, Austrade provides information to foreign businesses to encourage them to invest and operate in Australia. For example:

- research on industry capabilities and opportunities
- advice on market developments, trends and forecasts
- information on possible partners and competitors in the Australian market.

States also have agencies that provide information, advice and financial assistance. In WA the Department of State Development offers the following services:

- Information on business requirements, economic trends, trade and market analysis
- Identifying business opportunities and facilitating company networking
- Advice on market entry strategies
- Introductions to relevant government agencies and stakeholders

- Recommendations and contacts for regulators, industry partners, associations and supply chain networks

There is also a tax incentive for research and development (R & D). The Australian Government provides incentives for companies engaging in research and development. The R & D tax incentive provides companies with a tax offset for expenditure on R & D activities which may include activities conducted overseas.

Export Finance and Insurance Corporation (EFIC) Export Finance Guarantee

An export finance guarantee is a facility between EFIC, a bank or other financial institution and a foreign business partner. The EFIC provides a guarantee to the bank for the buyer's payment obligations. This secures finance and minimises the risk of payments not being made between businesses in different countries. This increased certainty encourages Australian businesses to venture overseas.

Home-grown benefits

For a business to have international success they must have a strong base. A business can use a strong domestic foundation to expand overseas. Marketing strategies can be tested, products developed and distribution channels established. Domestic success also establishes business systems in communication, administration and continuous improvement.

Sustainable revenue and profitability in domestic markets provides the finances needed to expand into international markets.

GLOBAL BUSINESS ETHICS

Investors, consumers, governments and the community all expect businesses to act ethically. It is not enough for a business to make profit. Businesses are expected to be good global citizens and use their economic and social influence to raise living standards domestically and globally.

Offshore labour

As free trade agreements deregulate labour markets workers can become more vulnerable to exploitation. A globalised economy results in the expensive sports shoes or denim jeans bought in Australia being made in sweatshops overseas. A sweatshop is a workplace where people work long hours for little pay in unhealthy conditions, usually making consumer items sold for high prices in developed nations. Sweatshops exist in all countries around the world.

Sweatshops are used to reduce costs and increase profit because workers are paid little for their work. Workers are forced to work unpaid overtime, with no breaks, and are punished for slow work and mistakes. The management of the large retail companies enjoy high salaries because of their decision to use sweatshop labour.

The ethical approach for global businesses relying on cheap labour working in poor conditions is to collaborate with local unions. Collaboration will put pressure on employers to raise wages and working conditions. Global businesses will continue to exploit workers to keep their profit margins. Are profits more important than human rights?

Unethical practice is seen in Australia when young people lose their jobs when they reach the age of adult wage rates. They may have a good work history and been a loyal employee over a number of years. It is cheaper for a business to replace them with a young worker on youth wage rates.

Ethics are based on judgements and personal experiences. Business owners and entrepreneurs must widen their experiences to understand the global business. If a business uses offshore labour it is a good idea for managers to visit the offshore partner to see the working conditions for themselves.

Part of doing business in a global marketplace is labour, jobs, moving to other countries. But it also means that skilled people will move to Australia.

Offshoring can also provide economic benefits and brand awareness in other countries. Selling goods and services in other countries supplements domestic revenue and there may be lower manufacturing and distribution costs. Building a global brand will also increase brand awareness in Australia.

If a business cannot find the specialised workers they need in Australia, the skill shortage can be filled by foreign workers.

Arguments against offshoring include:

- the decrease in employment in Australia as jobs are exported
- customers perhaps resenting having to deal with offshore customer service staff and overseas call centres
- it being more difficult for Australian businesses to manage offshore staff.

Environmental responsibility

Sustainability aims to meet the needs of corporate stakeholders today while seeking to protect and preserve resources and the environment for the future. Many Australian businesses and organisations are responding by managing their environmental impact. This includes reducing use and waste, and recycling of resources such as water, energy and paper. Companies are also measuring their carbon footprint and investigating carbon offsets.

The motivation is not all altruistic. Businesses can benefit from being sustainable in the following ways.

Reduced costs

Being more efficient with resources, recycling supplies and reducing waste results in a reduction in costs.

Staff loyalty

A 'green' building that uses more natural methods of lighting, heating and cooling is a healthier environment. Employees will also feel they are contributing to society by working in a sustainable business. Sustainable businesses have been shown to improve staff morale, increase staff productivity and reduce absenteeism.

Public relations and public image

Sustainable practices can differentiate a business in the market and be used to promote the business in a positive light. People will choose to patronise and invest in a business based on their commitment to the environment.

Carbon trading

An Emissions Trading Scheme (ETS) is a market based policy to encourage companies to reduce their greenhouse gas emissions. A form of an ETS is called a cap and trade. For example, the Federal Government places a cap on the total amount of emissions in Australia. If a company reduces their emissions below the cap they get credits. If another company needs to produce emissions above the cap they must buy credits from companies that pollute less. Over time the government lowers the cap to achieve a long-term national emissions target.

An ethical dilemma for business owners and managers exists because of different environmental regulations in different countries. An Australian business may be able to save money and manufacture goods or mine resources at a lower cost in a country which does not have the level of environmental protection as in Australia. Should that business exploit the weaker protection regime for profit while they damage the environment?

The ethics of the impact of business on the environment is important. A decision by a company that has negative impacts on the environment, not only affects them but the consequences can damage the wider environment, for example biological systems, the water table or the survival of a species.

Companies and governments see coal seam gas as having great potential as a source of energy and revenue. The 'fracking' process that is used to extract the gas pollutes the underground aquifers that are the source of much of our water. Fracking injects a mixture of sand, water and chemicals into underground rock at high pressure. The chemicals used during drilling are known to produce health effects and may contribute to systemic illness and cancer. The ethical dilemma is that this resource industry can generate income for companies and income for governments through taxes and royalties, employment and investment, but there are health and environmental impacts that are serious and long-lasting.

A leak off the northern coast of Western Australia...

Off the Kimberley coast of WA, an oil rig had an oil spill that lasted over 10 weeks and pumped out 400 barrels of oil a day according to the company. The oil spill could have been prevented if correct planning and safety management was conducted. The oil company chose to try and save money and time by drilling multiple wells quickly and did not install a cap on the well that starting pumping oil into the environment.

Outsourcing

Outsourcing involves an organisation identifying activities that can be given to another organisation (the vendor) to perform on their behalf. Instead of a company maintaining manufacturing, market research, administration or customer service operations these are provided by a third party for a fee. Outsourcing overseas is attractive because Australian companies can take advantage of lower pay and conditions in other countries.

A company can benefit from outsourcing because they are using a business that specialises in a particular function; it may have expertise that the company does not have. Other reasons to outsource functions are:

- lowering costs
- management being able to focus on core business activities
- avoiding costly investments in technology (information, manufacturing)
- improving customer focus.

Costs are also easier to manage. A company pays fixed and variable costs associated with maintaining facilities for employees, wages, superannuation and training. If an activity is outsourced there is one set fee that is much easier to plan for in the budget.

An additional benefit is increased workforce flexibility. A business may experience seasonal fluctuations in demand or other changing circumstances. It is easier and quicker to change arrangements with an outsourcing vendor as required.

YouTube
Ethical issues faced by international businesses

Dumping

Countries have different regulatory regimes covering product safety. Dumping involves selling products that are considered unsafe or unhealthy in countries that do not have the same product safety laws as the home country. For example, a product is deemed unsafe by Product Safety Australia and recalled or prohibited in Australia. The business now has stock that they cannot sell in Australia. The business will look to markets overseas that have not banned the product and sell it there. This can also happen within a country.

There is a clear ethical issue. A company will be concerned with the loss associated with not being able to sell its inventory and the cost associated with the disposal of illegal stock. There may be an opportunity to sell the products overseas. Should a company sell a product that has been deemed unsafe and banned at all? An ethical approach would be to explore alternatives to dumping, such as product improvements or modifications or at least providing additional information with the product to make consumers aware of the risks involved in the use of the product.

Fair trade

Businesses in the developed world are able to lower costs and increase profits by using cheap labour and sourcing materials and products at low prices. This benefits them but does not provide the means for the poorer country to improve their standard of living.

Fair trade is a label given to products, organisations and businesses that are committed to providing decent working conditions, sustainability and better terms of trade for farmers and workers in the developing world.

Fairtrade is an organisation that works to set fair prices for farmers and producers, improve working conditions and educate farmers about sustainable farming methods. The aim of Fairtrade is to encourage businesses to pay a fair and stable price to suppliers in developing countries and for governments to use legislation to improve and protect the rights of workers. For a product to have a Fairtrade label it must meet international standards set by the Fairtrade Labelling Organisations International (FLO).

OTHER ETHICAL DILEMMAS

Globalisation creates another dimension for ethical questions and business decisions. It also provides an opportunity for Australian businesses to take a positive stance on issues of ethical behavior, social responsibility, working conditions and environmental protection around the world.

Managing across borders includes difficult ethical dilemmas. The dilemma is between doing what is best for the company and its profit and doing what is best for the community, both local and global.

For example, Nestle uses genetically modified (GM) ingredients in its food products. It has been accused of dumping products rejected in Europe under GM laws, in developing Asian countries where the laws on GM products were either absent or less stringent.

Nestle launched bottled water in countries, such as Pakistan and India, that do not have widespread supplies of clean drinking water. Nestle sold safe clean water but priced it so high that it was unaffordable for the lower income groups. It turned water into a luxury item.

Another example is bribes. Corrupt politicians and government officials may request amounts of money in order for an Australian business to operate in their country. Do we see the bribes as a necessary cost of business or take a stand against corruption?

Reasons why business will pay bribes include:

- Competitors are giving bribes to obtain business.
- This is an accepted practice in the country.
- Tax laws of the country encourage bribery by writing it off as a business expense.
- The government has control over business activities – no bribe no business.
- Government officials are poorly paid and use bribery to supplement salaries.
- Bureaucratic delays can be costly for business.

An example involved the Australian Government and the Australian Wheat Board (AWB). While Saddam Hussein was in power in Iraq the United Nations imposed trade sanctions. The aim of prohibiting trade with Iraq was to pressure Hussein to stop his invasion of Kuwait. The Australian Government, through the AWB, paid bribes to the Iraqi Government to obtain wheat contracts in contravention of the sanctions.

CHAPTER 3
Free trade agreements

'World can run without money and currencies
but not without business and trade.'
– Amit Kalantri –

FREE TRADE AGREEMENTS

Governments support business growth and expansion overseas because it increases the nation's Gross Domestic Product (GDP). Jobs are created and governments collect more taxes, duties and fees. The nation's wealth increases, which should result in an increase in the standard of living for all Australians.

Successive Australian governments have standardised laws and regulations and introduced self-regulation. The goal is to increase the profit and efficiency of the private sector by reducing the time and money spent on complying with different laws in the different states and territories they operate in. A similar process is ongoing on a global scale. Domestically it means that states have the same laws and regulations. Globally national governments negotiate a standardisation of laws and regulations between countries.

Trade negotiations result in governments committing to free trade agreements. Free trade agreements are made between countries and to form trading regions. Australia has signed a range of trade agreements that regulate business operating globally. Trade agreements undergo a process of periodic review and negotiation.

An example of a free trade agreement is one involving tariffs and customs duties on agricultural products like wheat or apples. Two or more countries agree to standardise customs duties and tariffs, to reduce them or remove them. This means that each country can export their produce to other countries and sell it at a similar price as local produce.

Another example is the standardisation of policy regulating pharmaceuticals. Governments have a scheme where some medications are subsidised by governments to make them cheaper and easily accessible. The medications still have a high price but the government pays most of it. Countries agree to put the same medications on the subsidy list to make them easier to buy and fund the global expansion of pharmaceutical companies.

As part of free trade negotiations the US government seeks to extend the rights of US drug companies to charge high prices for medicines for longer periods. US proposals also undermine Australia's Pharmaceutical Benefits Scheme by requiring wholesale prices paid to drug companies to be based on market prices, rather than the existing process of comparison with similar, but lower cost, drugs.

YouTube
FREE TRADE || Korea-Australia agreement details

Another proposal by the US is to give US companies operating in other countries the right to sue governments over policies and laws that affect their sales and profits. For example, US tobacco companies could sue the Australian government for losses that result from Australia's plain packaging laws for cigarettes.

Free trade agreements can create opportunities for Australian exporters and investors to expand their businesses into overseas markets. They can provide access to overseas markets in all areas of trade such as goods, services and investment. Access to markets and the reduction in tariffs increases the competitiveness of Australian businesses. As part of any free trade agreement, Australia must remove trade barriers to make it easier and less expensive for imports.

Reducing trade barriers improves outcomes for consumers because it gives them easier access to more choice and lower prices. It also increases competitive pressures on domestic industry. Australian businesses now have to also compete with foreign businesses on a level playing field. This pressure motivates business people to innovate and improve efficiency in order to survive.

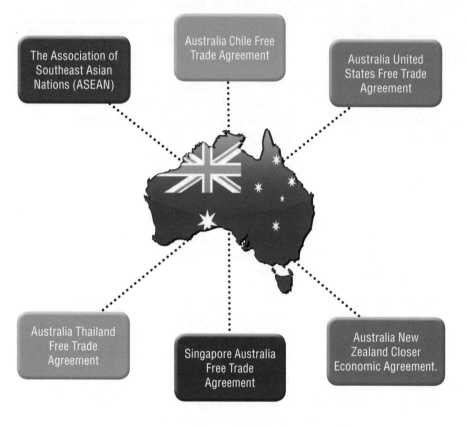

BUSINESS CONCEPTS

An FTA between Australia and Thailand resulted in growth in Australian exports. Trade barriers between the two countries were reduced. In practical terms it means that under the agreement thousands of products had their tariffs removed. An FTA between Australia and the US includes the removal of tariffs from a range of products, the removal of customs duties from digital products and a change in Australian copyright law to align it with US policy.

YouTube
Corporations 101:
What Are Free Trade
Agreements?

Figure 3.1: Australia is party to free trade agreements

China-Australia Free Trade Agreement

Prime Minister Abbott and President Xi concluded negotiations for the China-Australia Free Trade Agreement (ChAFTA) on 17 November 2014. It is planned to come into effect in 2015.

Some of the deregulation involved in ChAFTA includes:

- the removal of all tariffs on our dairy products within four to 11 years
- the removal of tariffs of 12 to 25 percent on beef over nine years
- the removal of tariffs on live animal exports within four years
- the removal of tariffs on sheep meat over eight years
- the removal of tariffs on wine over four years
- the removal of tariffs on all horticulture products within four years
- the immediate elimination of the three per cent tariff on barley
- the removal of tariffs across a range of processed foods including fruit juice and honey
- the removal of tariffs on all resources and energy products
- the removal of tariffs on transformed resources and energy products
- the removal of tariffs of up to 10 per cent on pharmaceuticals
- the removal of tariffs within four years for other manufactured products.

The Free Trade Agreement also covers services such as; legal, financial, education and health services.

The removal of tariffs means that the price of Australian goods and services will be lower when they are sold in China. This makes Australian goods and services more competitive against locally produced goods and services in China.

> **INNOVATIONS AND OPERATIONS**
>
> In 2013; agriculture and processed food was worth around $9 billion to Australian farmers and the broader agricultural sector, Australia exported over $85 billion worth of resources, energy and manufactured products to China and China was Australia's largest services market with exports in services valued at $7 billion.

> **Tariff:** a government charge on imports to increase the price of imported goods and services. The aim is to protect local businesses by making imports more expensive.

ASEAN-Australia-New Zealand Free Trade Agreement (AANZFTA)

The AANZFTA involves the ASEAN (Association of Southeast Asian Nations) countries of Brunei, Myanmar, Cambodia, Indonesia, Laos, Malaysia, the Philippines, Singapore, Thailand and Vietnam. It commenced on 1 January 2010. It covers the industry sectors of goods, services, investment and intellectual property.

Key points include:

- Eliminate tariffs on 96% of Australia's exports to ASEAN nations by 2020.
- AANZFTA-certified goods have their tariffs reduced when they enter ASEAN countries.
- International arbitration is established to resolve foreign investment disputes.
- The FTA sets minimum standards for the treatment of foreign investors and their investments within signatory countries.

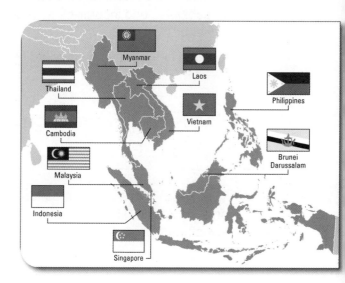

For example:

- **meat and livestock:** tariffs on most meat tariff lines phased to 0% and access for live bovine imports guaranteed
- **dairy products:** tariffs phased to 0% except for a few products Indonesia, the Philippines and Malaysia
- **iron and steel:** tariffs on a majority of products phased to 0% or to 10% or less
- **new passenger motor vehicles:** elimination of all tariffs in the Philippines.

Investment protections under the AANZFTA include:

- Allow funds of an investor to be transferred freely and without delay.

- Ensure that investors receive prompt, adequate and effective compensation in the event of expropriation or nationalisation of an investment.

- Investors may refer disputes about alleged breaches of these obligations to international arbitration.

Australia New Zealand Closer Economic Relations Trade Agreement (ANZCERTA)

The Australia-New Zealand Closer Economic Relations Trade Agreement (ANZCERTA) is a bilateral free trade agreement that covers all trans-Tasman trade in goods, including agricultural products and services. It took effect in January 1983.

Key points include:

- All tariffs and restrictions on import and export between the two countries are prohibited.

- Minimise government industry assistance and export subsidies and incentives to ensure a level playing field.

- Food standards are standardised.

INNOVATIONS AND OPERATIONS

Trade between Australia and New Zealand in 2013 amounted to: $21,554 billion.

Two-way investment between Australia and New Zealand is worth more than $110 billion.

Pacific Agreement on Closer Economic Relations-Plus (PACER-Plus)

The PACER-Plus is a proposed free trade agreement between Australia, New Zealand and 14 Pacific Island countries that would cover trade in goods, services and foreign investment.

An issue with a Pacific free trade agreement is its impact on revenues of member Pacific islands. Pacific governments already struggle to provide public services like health, education, clean water, police and emergency services. An important source of funds for spending on these services comes from the taxes on imported goods. If the PACER-Plus is signed it would remove these tariffs and greatly reduce the revenue Pacific island governments rely on to fund public services.

It has been estimated that Fiji, Papua New Guinea, Samoa and Vanuatu stand to lose about $10 million from tariff cuts on Australian and New Zealand imports.

Unity groups are also concerned about the lack of public consultation and public information concerning the negotiation of PACER-Plus. They would prefer the negotiations were suspended until communities were consulted and there was more research on the impact of a free trade agreement on Pacific island economies.

CHAPTER 4
E-commerce

'The first rule of any technology used in a business is that automation applied to an efficient operation will magnify the efficiency. The second is that automation applied to an inefficient operation will magnify the inefficiency.'

– Bill Gates –

Global business grew because of the development of transport and communication systems over the world. Technologies today have created a business environment with secure payment systems, around the clock access to online shopping and the digital distribution of products. Currency conversions are automated, language can be translated and payments and communications are protected by encryption.

Technology has created new industries and business opportunities for global expansion; specialised technologies such as nanotechnology and biotechnology. Technology enables people and companies to provide their goods and services around the world. Australian businesses reduce costs by using administrative staff in Asia linked by email and groupware. A graphic design artist in Australia sends their designs to clients around the world.

ONLINE AND DIGITAL TECHNOLOGIES

A website gives customers access to the business all the time from anywhere in the world. Customer orders on a website can be linked to delivery and payment systems. It can be difficult for staff to keep up with emails and online orders but automated processes can help staff cope with the demand. There is free or low-cost online design, word processing and spreadsheet software that businesses can use that is much cheaper than buying software licences. The Internet can be used to research businesses and markets to gather business intelligence. With broadband large files such as contracts, software and designs can be distributed quickly and securely and web conferencing can occur. Mobile devices such as phones, laptops and digital assistants can facilitate better communication with staff, customers and suppliers.

eBusiness

This refers to a business built on the use of information and communication technologies (ICT). Selling products and services online may help you save on costs, reach more customers and be able to complete orders and projects in a shorter time. Online, your business is available 24 hours a day seven days a week. This is good for sales but it can also be difficult to keep up with demand and customer communications. There are many different ways businesses operate using ebusiness and these are outlined here.

eBusiness methods

Communicate with customers, clients and suppliers via email and SMS. Send emails to other businesses to order products and services. Sell products or services via a website. Use the Web to find information such as prices, phone numbers and reviews of products. Staff work at home and keep in touch with the business online. Use the Web for research such as the latest industry trends. Use the Internet for online banking and to pay bills.

> **BUSINESS IN SOCIETY**
> In 2005 the ABS found that 89% of all businesses had computers, 77% had internet access and 27% had a website. In 2005 40% of all businesses received income from orders placed via the Internet, earning a total of $39.6 billion from e-business.

M-commerce

YouTube
Wishpond Webinar: Evolution of Commerce

An emerging technology is based on the use of wireless mobile devices to conduct business over a high-speed Internet connection. It is called mobile commerce or m-commerce. It is the combination of a mobile phone, a **WAP Internet connection** and a payment system. A mobile phone will become an electronic wallet. This is predicted to grow because of the increased capability of the mobile network.

> **WAP:** Wireless application protocol; a technology that allows mobile phones to connect to the Internet with specially coded webpages.

It has been happening already with mobile phone users being able to pay for and download ring tones, wallpapers and games and to vote for reality TV shows, but the plan is to extend the technology to all sorts of products and services.

Some issues of concern have been identified with m-commerce:

- **Spam and scams:** m-commerce provides another platform for inboxes to be filled with unwanted and fraudulent messages.

- **Privacy:** businesses will be able to collect even more personal information from customers.

- **Informed consumers:** because of the screen size of mobile phones and memory limits customers may not be able see the full terms and conditions of sale or the details of complaints and returns processes before making a purchase.

> **INNOVATION AND ENTERPRISE**
> PayPal Australia provides check-out services to more than 100,000 local merchants with more than 5.5 million customers. PayPal has opened an m-commerce service in Australia called PayPal Express Checkout. Express Checkout on mobile devices runs in mobile browsers with pages optimised for smaller mobile screens and mobile keyboards.
>
> Visa also launched a mobile wallet where users can complete a payment with Visa Checkout without leaving the shop's website.

- **Consumer debt:** because of how easy it is to use and access, and any hidden charges from mobile phone and Internet providers, consumers may get caught in high levels of debt.

In the future, sales and revenues generated online and mobile platforms will increase. Retailers will use smartphone apps, websites and portals designed for tablets. The integration of secure payment systems into websites and apps makes it easier for customers to make purchases.

Brands use technology to embrace new channels and approaches to global expansion. Businesses and brands use multiple approaches to sell their products. Businesses use the traditional bricks and mortar approach and supplement it with websites to offer products and services to global customers. Businesses sell online, use international shipping and participate in global marketplaces.

M-commerce makes it easier to enter new markets. In the past, retailers would have to build relationships with dozens of different wholesalers and distributors to get their business off the ground. Online technologies allow businesses to have a market presence without having to set up infrastructure first.

But m-commerce is no guarantee for profit and success. To set up and maintain a web presence, promote online services and manage distribution is costly. Businesses must keep spending substantial amounts for promotion to maintain awareness of and interest in their website and online offerings. Maintaining an online presence and social media profile requires full-time staff and a large promotion budget. Multiple platforms must be maintained – social media, website, apps and search engine optimisation.

For success retailers must:

- **Optimise tablet and smartphone experience:** offer an app or website that is designed for tablets and smartphones and integrate shopping carts and payment systems.

- **Use social media and mobile marketing to drive store traffic:** use SMS, Facebook and Twitter to promote sales, distribute discount coupons and invite customers to events and exclusive in store offers.

- **Provide exceptional service:** include stock availability information online, use shopping histories to suggest products and provide product personalisation.

E-commerce strategies

An e-commerce strategy should support the business as a whole. It can be a costly venture and it should be considered carefully because e-commerce failure may have an impact on overall profitability and survival.

Examples of strategies that use e-commerce for global business are listed to follow.

International shipping

This strategy is adding international shipping to an existing domestic website. Capturing market share is difficult without major investment in marketing campaigns in target countries.

Branded website

A business may build on existing exporting trade with a website and online sales. It is a way to increase brand awareness and demand, and provide product information. This method is often used by retailers that already operate in stores internationally.

Wholesale online

This refers to partnering with a business in another country, using their established infrastructure, customer base and distribution channels. In this case the website would target retailers such as department stores instead of targeting consumers directly.

Local market URL

To build a strong presence in a new overseas market a business may develop and maintain a website in the foreign country. Instead of com.au the website would have com. eu, com.uk or com.nz. This creates an impression of a local business, one committed to the local market, not a foreign company trying to compete with domestic brands. The website would be in the local language, currency and reflect the culture.

CHAPTER 5
Unit 3 Environment activities

'A day will come when there will be no battlefields,
but markets opening to commerce
and minds opening to ideas.'
– Victor Hugo –

Topic study

1. What are two reasons in favour of globalisation?
2. What are two reasons against globalisation?
3. Discuss two reasons why businesses consider global growth.
4. Why is a low-cost country advantageous for global growth?
5. Explain two technologies a business could use for global growth.
6. What is offshoring?
7. Why do businesses use tax havens?
8. How does Austrade assist businesses wanting to expand overseas?
9. What is the role of the World Trade Organisation?
10. What is dumping?
11. Discuss the ethical dilemma involved with offshore labour.
12. Discuss the ethical dilemma involved with environmental responsibility.
13. What is a free trade agreement (FTA)?
14. List three examples of FTAs Australia is part of.
15. How can the removal of tariffs assist Australian businesses overseas?
16. What is m-commerce?
17. What are two examples of eBusiness methods?
18. What are two concerns that have been identified with m-commerce?
19. What are two examples of e-commerce strategies?
20. What is e-commerce?

Business research

1. Strategic alliances

Research the following forms of strategic alliance. Explain how they work, and the advantages and disadvantages of the form. Find examples of each form. Choose one form and suggest a possible alliance involving companies you are aware of in Australia and globally.

- Merger
- Joint venture
- Franchise

2. Global business: role of ethics

There is a concern about a form of business called 'fast fashion'. Research fast fashion and describe the ethical concerns about the industry. Describe examples of fast fashion and how they operate.

3. Free trade agreements

Australia is a party to the Trans Pacific Partnership (TPP) which aims to create a free trade zone in the Asia Pacific region.

i. Who are the 12 countries involved in the TPP?
ii. What are some products or industries the TPP will cover?
iii. How could Australia benefit from the TPP?
iv. What are some concerns regarding the TPP?

4. Investor State Dispute Settlements

One area of the TPP (and other free trade agreements) is Investor State Dispute Settlement (ISDS).

i. How does ISDS work?
ii. Why could this be a concern to Australia?
iii. Discuss a recent case involving ISDS and Australia

5. The role of e-commerce and free trade agreements

Many countries including Australia have a consumption based tax. In Australia it is the Goods and Services Tax (GST), in the UK it is the Value Added Tax (VAT). Governments charge the tax on online purchases even though the goods are imported from other countries. In Australia the GST applies to all online purchases over $1000. The Federal Government can negotiate with the States to reduce the threshhold.

i. Make a list of the consumption tax rates of 10 countries including Australia and its trading partners.

ii. Find what the online threshholds are of those countries.

If the threshhold is reduced to $20, for example:

i.   What impact could it have on consumption patterns?

ii. Discuss whether Australian businesses would benefit from the law change.

iii. Is this something that could be part of a free trade agreement? Choose an FTA that Australia is party to and suggest a rate and threshhold.

Response

1. Global business – role of ethics

Walmart bribed bureaucrats in Mexico to expedite building permits that enabled the company to expand rapidly. The alleged bribes totaled more than $8 million. Politicians and government officials may request amounts of money in order for an Australian business to operate in their country.

i.   Why are payments like these seen as a necessary cost of business?

ii. Why is it an ethical dilemma for global business growth?

iii. Find two recent examples.

2. Tax minimisation

In Australia, nine of the biggest global drug companies made $8 billion in revenue. Through transfer pricing they ended up paying $85 million in tax, an effective tax rate of 1%. Executives representing the nine companies have stated that they obey all Australian and international tax laws.

i.   What is the strategy used by the companies called?

ii. Explain how it works.

iii. Discuss the ethical dilemma in using this strategy.

3. Free trade agreements

Recently there was a recall of clothing in Australia based on concerns about Azo dyes. Research the topic of product safety regarding Azo dyes in Australia.

i.   Why are Azo dyes a product safety concern?

ii. What companies in Australia have been involved in recalls and regulatory actions?

iii. What implications are there for free trade agreements involving Australia?

4. The role of e-commerce

In a small group develop an e-commerce plan for an Australian business. The plan is to maintain bricks and mortar outlets in Australia and offer online shopping for international customers.

The business can be local or a national enterprise. Divide the work equally and prepare a written plan and a summary group presentation. Work can be divided on a task basis.

The tasks are to:

- Research the topic and find key points.
- Make recommendations based on what you have learned.
- Discuss how you made your decisions by comparing options.

As a group:

i.   Discuss e-commerce options and decide on a plan and tools to expand internationally

ii.   Develop a summary presentation.

    a.   Describe the business you have chosen, their products, services and their target markets.

    b.   Describe the e-commerce strategies the company could use to expand globally; what they are; and how they would work and the benefits to the company.

    c.   Design how e-commerce tools could look, such as a home page, online advertising, payment page, product catalogue and pricing, app, or social media profile page.

    d.   Discuss what incentives Australian governments could give the business, examples of compliance needs with laws in other countries, and if there are free trade agreements that could have an impact on them.

A suggested format for your e-commerce plan is:

> **Introduction**
> a. above
>
> **E-commerce plan**
> b. above
>
> **E-commerce designs**
> c. above
>
> **Business environment: macro**
> d. above

5. Impact of globalisation

'The study of international business is fine if you are going to work in a large multinational enterprise, but it has no relevance for individuals who are going to work in small firms.' Discuss this statement.

6. Global business: role of ethics

An Australia executive visits their foreign subsidiary in a developing nation. She finds that they have hired a 12-year-old girl to work on the factory floor, in violation of the company's prohibition on child labour. She tells the local manager to replace the child so she can go back to school. The local manager tells the Australian executive that the child is an orphan, with no other means of support and she will probably become a street child if she is denied work. What should the Australian executive do?

The 4 Plan

Using a plan to organise your work will focus you on your main tasks and make your research more efficient.

- Introduction: identify the topic, theme or purpose of your presentation and list four key points or aspects of the topic.

- For each key point or aspect list the Boolean search terms you will use to find information.

- Record two or more sources for each point to show what you read to learn about them.

- Make recommendations based on what you have learned.

Introduction

Sources | **Sources** | **Sources** | **Sources**

Recommendations

CHAPTER 6
Global growth

'Globalisation is a fact of economic life.'
– Carlos Salinas de Gortari –

A GLOBAL BRAND

When entering an overseas market businesses have the options of:

- standardising their marketing mix or
- adapting the marketing mix to the local preferences and market characteristics.

Some businesses aim to build a global brand with a standardised marketing approach throughout the world. Global branding requires large budgets but the use of technology such as websites and social media can make global campaigns affordable for businesses all sizes.

The benefits of a global brand

Consistency

Global branding enables a business to communicate consistent messages to customers in all markets. This can result in stronger brand awareness and positioning as all marketing supports the same message.

Low risk

Businesses can use marketing strategies that have worked in domestic markets such as promotions and advertising.

Lower cost

A business will be able to achieve economies of scale by using the same advertising and packaging throughout the world. Multiple teams for research and marketing strategy are not needed. A centralised team of people will develop marketing strategies for all markets.

There may be some updating for different languages but it will be quicker and less expensive to use the same approaches in all markets. Costs rise if different marketing strategies are required in different countries or regions, for example separate campaigns with different packaging, product names, slogans and advertising campaigns.

Easier to manage

A standardised approach to global branding will be less complex than working with multiple advertising agencies, marketing teams and different strategies.

Better differentiation

A consistent global brand will stand out from the competition more than a business that tries to blend in with domestic businesses. Everywhere a consumer travels they will see the same logo, colours, product names and advertising.

When to go global

An important part of planning a business venture is to assess its feasibility. Feasibility is about the potential of a market. Will it provide a level of sales that will result in profit? Will it provide sustainable profit over the medium to long term?

Feasibility analysis includes:

- assessing the total market size
- assessing competitors in the target market
- assessing capital requirements to launch and sustain the business
- considering the experience and expertise of staff and partners.

A business may have great staff, a product in demand and established channels domestically, but will it work on the global stage?

Other factors to consider when deciding to go global include the following:

Level of consumer demand

To assess feasibility, the size of consumer demand must be estimated. Estimate the total demand for the same or similar products and the possible market share that could be captured.

Part of estimating demand is forecasting demand over time and considering economic characteristics that have an impact on demand. These include interest rate and inflation settings, unemployment levels, exchange rates and economic growth. Current settings and possible future changes should be evaluated.

A business may hire a research company to undertake marketing analysis, ideally in the market they are targeting.

Consumption patterns

There may be political motivations behind consumption patterns in some countries or regions. A company and its products may be boycotted because of their business practices such as animal testing, sexist or racist advertising. This may present an opportunity for a competitor to step in and capture the lost market share.

In developing countries there can be a change in consumption patterns. A country may grow in wealth and there may be a new middle class of people who have higher wages and more discretionary income.

A result of growth in developing economies such as India and China, is the increase in living standards and spending for an increasing part of the population. Even just the seemingly small transition from 'poverty' to 'adequate food and clothing' results in great demand for different products and a significant change in consumption patterns. There are also parts of the population that are reaching a high middle class standard of living. These segments of the population are demanding products and services such as high-nutrient food, larger homes, cars, health care, education and other services.

China's consumption patterns have changed remarkably in recent years. Chinese people now spend proportionately less on basic daily necessities and more on travel, IT products, housing, medical insurance, entertainment and education.

L'Oreal purchased Yue Sai, a Chinese cosmetics company, in 2004. They are now positioning it as a luxury cosmetics brand. Ingredients from Chinese traditions have been included in the products.

In Western countries there have been two changes in food consumption patterns. There has been a rise in demand for processed, packaged foods for value and convenience and also a rise in 'healthy' products that target a range of health issues such as gluten intolerance, heart disease and weight loss. Analysis should also include seasonal patterns in consumption or peaks and troughs around holidays and cultural events.

Social media is a useful source for information about changes in consumption patterns. Businesses should monitor social media to follow conversations about brands and consumer preferences to predict the types of products that are regarded as desirable, part of a fad or have become a trend.

Competitor activity

A competitor analysis is an important part of assessing the feasibility of a global venture. To gain an understanding of the target market, it is vital to have thorough understanding of the competition. The better that you understand competitors, the more effective marketing strategies will be.

Global business increases competition. When identifying competitors a business must include exporters, local businesses and online sellers.

It can be difficult to assess competition in a foreign country. A research company in the target country is a good source of primary data regarding competitors.

Information can be:

- **Primary data:** based on research and observation, it may involve extensive time spent in the target country conducting market research and includes exploring competitor websites, outlets, patents and pricing.

- **Secondary data:** this is available in published form and includes government publications, trade shows, media reports, advertising, competitor annual reports and product brochures.

- **Anecdotal data:** comes from discussions with suppliers, customers and past employees of competitors.

Competitor activity that supports market entry includes:	Competitor activity that makes it difficult for market entry includes:
• few competitors • products that are easily copied or substituted • customers unsatisfied with products on offer • competitors not offering choice or value for money • competitors missing a market need or niche market.	• size, market dominance and wealth of competitors (can they outlast others in a price war?) • that they are an established brand that is part of the country's culture • established distribution channels with strong working relationships with suppliers and retailers

Adapting strategies for international markets

A business conducts international market research and is aware of the differences between international markets to devise better marketing strategies. The differences between markets has an impact on the design and implementation of strategies and form the basis of the identification of target markets.

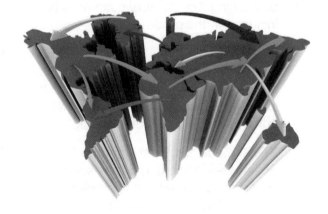

Adapting marketing strategies increases the costs involved in strategy implementation. It is less expensive to standardise strategies across foreign markets, but treating markets as homogenous may result in marketing failure.

Approaches to strategy adaptation are:

- Use domestic strategies internationally with no change.
- Adapt strategies based on generalisations about a region, for example Europe, South East Asia.
- Adapt strategies to countries based on national market research.
- Adapt strategies to regions or target markets in countries based on market research

Standardisation or adaptation can be applied to the following elements of the marketing mix.

Positioning

In some cultures individualism and individual success are highly valued. Products are marketed based on the sense of achievement that comes from owning them. Positioning is based on consumers feeling they have 'made it' if they own a certain product.

Other cultures value collectivism and collective achievement highly so marketing that focuses on standing out and being better than others is not as effective.

Product features

Colours play a significant role in the design and marketing of products, packaging, branding and advertising. Different cultures place difference significance on colours. In Australia red is used in warnings and to signify danger, while in other cultures green or black are used. In Asia white is the colour of funerals, while white is the colour of weddings in Western cultures. Coca Cola has built global awareness of its red colour in its packaging and logo.

Differences in climate have an impact on marketing strategies. Climates create demand for products and services in some countries but not others with different climates. Product packaging and distribution methods may need to be adapted to different climates to prevent damage. Products made for a winter in Australia may not be suitable for winters in Europe, for example. An example is a washing machine manufacturer adapting the speed of their washing machines in Europe based on the amount of sunshine in each country. Washing machines sold in southern Europe, which has more sunshine, have slower spin cycles than washing machines sold in northern Europe.

The features of the product also include those set by common practice, laws and regulations. For example, different countries have different labelling rules and electrical requirements (appliances in the US should conform to 110 volts, in the UK 220 volts, ans they have different types of plugs).

In the 1950s Pepsi lost market share to Coca Cola in some Southeast Asia countries when it changed its vending machines from dark blue to a light blue. Light blue is a symbol of death and mourning in Southeast Asia.

In 2004, IKEA found that it needed to change the colours of its products to better target California's Latino population. After IKEA designers visited the homes of Hispanic staff, the Swedish furniture retailer realised the mostly black or white colour options were not bold enough for Latino tastes.

Process

The process aspect of the marketing mix will also need to be adapted to international markets. The use of online solutions, distribution networks and how staff communicate depend upon the level of infrastructure in a country and the level of Internet speed and use.

People

There may be a need for adaptation of the people aspect of the marketing mix. A business will decide on the mix of local and expatriate staff based on the supply of suitable labour in the target country. The business will have to conduct training programs to educate local staff in business processes and culture.

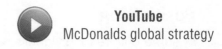

YouTube
McDonalds global strategy

Product name and slogans

Language and cultural differences need to be considered when deciding whether the same product name and slogan will be used or if it will be different in different countries.

Coca Cola standardise their product name in all markets using the same font and wavy pattern and colour (red). Even if consumers cannot read English they can recognise the brand.

Following are examples of businesses that got it wrong:

- Colgate introduced a toothpaste in France called 'Cue' which is the name of a well-known pornographic magazine there.

- In Italy a campaign for 'Schweppes Tonic Water' translated the name into 'Schweppes Toilet Water'.

- Clairol introduced the 'Mist Stick', a curling iron, into Germany where 'mist' is slang for manure.

- When Ford sold their Pinto in Brazil they discovered Pinto was Brazilian slang for 'tiny male genitals'. Ford renamed the car the Corcel meaning 'horse'.

- When General Motors sold the Chevy Nova in South America, it was unaware that 'no va' means 'it won't go' in Spanish. GM renamed the car to Caribe.

Slogans are part of positioning and also depend on translations and language differences.

- In Chinese the 'Finger lickin' good' slogan of KFC translated into 'Eat your fingers off'.

- In Spain, when Coors Brewing translated its slogan 'Turn it loose' into Spanish it became 'Suffer from diarrhea'.

- Pepsi's 'Come alive with the Pepsi Generation' translated into 'Pepsi brings your ancestors back from the grave' in Chinese.

- Parker Pen marketed a ballpoint pen in Mexico with the slogan, 'It won't leak in your pocket and embarrass you'. They made a mistake with the Spanish translation and their ads stated, 'It won't leak in your pocket and make you pregnant'.

Some businesses fail or have difficulty with entering overseas markets because they have not done the research to understand the culture. A standardised approach may not be possible.

CHAPTER 7
Global alliances

'Few companies have everything that they need.
You may need money, customers, or product.
No matter what you need, there is someone who has it.
That someone is a potential corporate partner.'

– Curtis E Sahakian –

STRATEGIC ALLIANCES

A strategic alliance is when two or more businesses form a partnership for a project, business venture or for the long term to create a new business. Strategic alliance is a strategy of collaboration between businesses for mutual benefit. An alliance should bring income to alliance partners that would not otherwise occur.

The businesses in a strategic alliance share customers, resources, staff and operations. The aim for alliance partners is to create synergy in the alliance, to create a competitive advantage greater that they could have on their own.

Strategic alliances enable businesses to gain competitive advantage by sharing not only resources but also customer databases, target markets, knowledge, contacts, technologies, capital and people.

Small or new businesses form strategic alliances to benefit from access to the established channels of distribution, marketing and brand reputation of a larger established business. Established businesses enter alliances to increase their capability for geographic expansion, cost reduction and manufacturing. Strategic alliances are often formed between businesses that are based in different regions of the world.

Advantages of strategic alliances

Advantages of strategic alliances include:

- quick access to a new market
- reduction of competition by forming an alliance with competitors
- larger market share
- increased sales and income
- gaining new expertise and technology
- access to research and development for business development
- increase in the range of products and services

- the opportunity to share operating costs and working capital
- access to established distribution channels
- gaining greater knowledge of customs and culture in other countries and regions
- the opporunity to build greater global brand awareness.

Disadvantages of strategic alliances

Disadvantages of strategic alliances include:

- they may take on the weaknesses of the partner, for example a lack of management expertise, unmotivated staff or high costs
- less efficient communication in a larger multinational business
- increased conflict over decisions and allocation of business resources
- making the alliance work takes time and energy away from the core business activity
- loss of control over product quality, operating costs, employees and so on.

Types of strategic alliances

Outsourcing

Outsourcing is a strategy that involves using a company overseas to perform a business function. This is different to offshoring where companies use their own employees in locations around the world.

YouTube
Outsourcing: Is it good or bad?

A business in Australia can use an overseas company that specialises in a certain function. They have well-trained staff and efficient operations that can perform the function on a contract basis more cheaply than a company doing it themselves.

Examples of work Australian businesses are contracting overseas include game development, engineering and technical design, mobile app development, human resources and payroll.

An Australian business can access local knowledge and expertise by outsourcing legal functions in the target country. They may also be able to lower costs by using labour in countries that have lower wages and conditions.

Stable and reliable communications technology provides access to locations around the world. India is one of the largest providers of outsourcing services in the world. There, highly qualified, skilled, English speaking workers work for a fraction of the cost of people in Australia and other developed economies.

The impact on employment of outsourcing includes:

- employment lost in Australia as a result of moving functions offshore
- new jobs created in other countries.

The reduction in operating costs results in extra capital that can be used for business growth such as research and development, marketing and product development.

Acquisition

An acquisition provides a quicker start in exploiting an overseas market. A business buys another that has been operating.

Businesses acquire target businesses as a growth strategy because it can create a bigger, more competitive and more cost-efficient company. This exploits synergy; two businesses together are more valuable than they are apart, combining skills, expertise, technology, capital and market share.

When a target business is acquired it ceases to exist and becomes part of the purchasing business. Acquisitions are commonly made by buying a majority of company shares. Acquisitions can be either hostile or friendly.

1. Hostile acquisition

This is the acquisition of one company by another by going directly to the shareholders and making an offer to buy their shares or by using their voting power to place people on the board of directors to approve the acquisition. It is hostile because the purchase is attempted without the consent or approval of existing management and directors.

The purchasing company may:

- **use a tender offer:** propose to purchase majority shares at a fixed price above the current market price and motivate shareholders to sell their shares to them
- **buy shares on the open market:** buy enough shares through the stock exchange to control the company
- **use a proxy fight:** the purchaser persuades enough shareholders to vote to replace the management of the company with one which will approve the acquisition.

The bear hug

The 'bear hug' approach to a hostile takeover involves a buyer making an offer to the company's board to take over the company without approaching the shareholders. The proposed purchase and its offered share price is then made public. The aim is to put the 'squeeze' on the board of directors to accept an offer they may not like through shareholder pressure and media scrutiny.

YouTube
Hostile takeovers

2. Friendly acquisition

A friendly acquisition occurs when the purchase of majority shares is part of an agreed, negotiated process with consent of the board of directors and full disclosure to existing shareholders. In order for a purchaser to buy majority shares, existing shareholders may have to agree to sell their shares. It is more likely shareholders will accept the offer if it is a friendly acquisition.

A danger in acquisitions is paying too much for the target business. Management may see huge potential and the target business may be seen to provide market entry and market share that is valuable. But if too much is paid for it, the gains in sales and profit may not be enough to cover the purchase price and the repayments for debt used to fund the purchase.

Another important aspect is to bring something to the acquisition and not to totally rely on the purchased business for success. There must be technology, expertise or marketing strategies that will work to increase the success of the purchased business. This means that the acquisition will create a strong base that can be built on.

Mergers

A merger is when the shareholders of two companies become the shareholders of a new merged company. A merger is similar to an acquisition, but both companies involved are of a similar size and agree to form a new company. Rather than a purchase or takeover, it is an agreement between two companies.

It may involve a new name, logo and slogan to launch and identify the new company.

A merger can lead to job losses as there would be people doing the same jobs in the companies involved, such as human resources, accounting and marketing. There are also other rationalisations. Retail outlets or offices may be rebranded and some closed if the companies were operating in the same places before the merger. Asset sales may be carried out if there are double ups in equipment, buildings, vehicles and other assets. The hope is that this will lead to overall cost reductions and increased profits.

There are three main types of mergers and acquisitions: horizontal, vertical and conglomerate.

1. Horizontal merger

A **horizontal merger or acquisition** is when two companies in the same industry combine.

The South African company, Woolworths, purchased David Jones for $2.2 billion. Woolworths plan to use David Jones to sell some of their South African brands. Woolworths also have

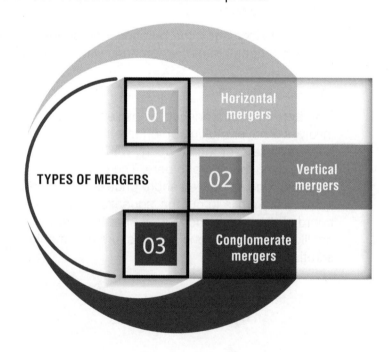

customer relationship management technology that will be used to refine the marketing strategies of David Jones.

2. Vertical merger

A **vertical merger or acquisition** occurs when a business buys or merges with one of its suppliers.

Owning a supplier can reduce operating costs and also increase competitive advantage. Control of a supplier can limit competitors' access to a product.

Ansell purchased two suppliers of gloves, BarrierSafe Solutions and Midas.

3. Conglomerate merger

A **conglomerate merger or acquisition** occurs between two unconnected companies.

A company may want to branch out into a different industry or market. The plan is to achieve this with lower risk by buying an established company. A company can maintain profits over seasonal and economic highs and lows because they own businesses in a range of industries.

Perth based company Wesfarmers owns businesses in a range of industries including coal mining, LPG, safety products, chemicals and industrial products and is now the owner of supermarket chain Coles, Bunnings, Target and Kmart.

Advantages of acquisitions or mergers include:

- high quality staff, additional skills and knowledge
- accessing funds and assets for business growth, eg. manufacturing and distribution facilities
- it may be less expensive to buy an established business than to expand
- accessing a wider customer base and increase market share
- diversification of products and services
- reducing operating costs through rationalisation
- reducing competition by buying competitors
- ownership of intellectual property.

Joint venture

A joint venture is an alliance where the businesses involved start up an independent company. The company is formed using the resources from all alliance partners and each partner owns a percentage of the joint venture company.

The venture partners usually form a new company for the joint venture. That way the company can focus on the joint venture project and the individual partners can still focus on their own core businesses.

It is a good idea to form a joint venture with a partner that is a local business in the target country. The local partner will have knowledge of the culture and consumer preferences. They will also have a working knowledge of laws and regulations, established distribution networks and experience with working with the local media and financial institutions.

Joint ventures often fail because of resistance to change and poor communication. Employees of all joint venture partners must be committed to making the arrangement work. They must understand the difficulties of the joint venture but also what they have to gain from it.

Sharing information is vital. Joint ventures also fail when the employees continue to see joint venture partners as a threat or as competition. All employees and businesses must exchange knowledge and expertise and establish good working relationships both formally and informally. Meetings, committees, joint business social events, employee 'swaps', teams made up of people from all partner businesses, and internal promotions will build a single vision and commitment to the success of the joint venture.

An example of a joint venture is the contract to build the LNG infrastructure on Barrow Island, off the North coast of WA, worth over $2 billion. Chevron awarded the Gorgon Project contract to a joint venture between CB&I and Kentz (CKJV). CB&I have a long history of design, fabrication and construction and Kentz brings engineering project management expertise.

Franchising

The International Franchise Association defines franchising as a:

> 'continuing relationship in which the franchisor provides a licensed privilege to do business, plus assistance in organising training, merchandising and management in return for a consideration from the franchisee'.

Other aspects that are included in a franchise business model include:

- products and services
- trademark
- business concept
- marketing strategies and plans
- operational standards and systems
- training
- quality control.

The franchisor is able to expand into global markets without having to invest its own capital. The franchisee gains through access to an established, proven business model and brand awareness which makes it a lower risk business venture.

International franchises are more difficult to manage, and ensure standards are maintained, because of the geographic distances, language barriers and different laws and regulations in different countries.

A company may form a relationship with a Master Franchisee in a country or region. The master franchisee acts on behalf of the franchisor to set up and fund new franchises. This can be more successful than the franchisor trying to manage new franchises from a location in another country. The master franchisee is located in the target country with knowledge of the local language, culture and business environment.

The benefit for a franchisor is increased global market access and global brand awareness at a lower cost than if they opened fully-owned stores with the added income of ongoing franchise fees and royalties.

Examples of strategic alliances

An alliance between Starbucks and United Airlines resulted in their coffee being offered on flights with the Starbucks logo on the cups. A partnership with Kraft foods resulted in Starbucks coffee being marketed in grocery stores in the US.

Examples of global franchises include; Subway, McDonalds, 7 Eleven, Baskin-Robbins, Hertz, Snap Fitness and many more.

Jeanswest began in Perth in 1972. Jeanswest operates 3,000 stores across Australia, New Zealand, South East Asia and the Middle East. They look for franchisees particularly in the southern hemisphere and provide support such as visual merchandising procedures, cost-effective store designs and bulk international orders where individual franchisees can save by combining their regional stock orders.

For about 30 years Ford and Mazda had a partnership and worked on joint projects where they worked together to design and construct vehicles. It came about primarily because of Mazda's financial problems. Ford's capital and ownership (up to 33% at its peak in the 1990s) meant that Mazda could survive. Now that Mazda is operating strongly, Ford's ownership has been reduced to 2%. By working together Ford and Mazda were able to save tens of millions of dollars in research and development costs.

Tasmanian bootmaker, Blundstone, moved its manufacturing to Asia. The savings in costs stopped Blundstone from going out of business.

Australian companies such as Telstra offshore to lower-cost locations such as India and the Philippines. The ANZ bank has call centres in Australia, New Zealand, Manila and Bangalore, but all staff are ANZ employees.

Starting a strategic alliance

An alliance is worthwhile if it benefits all partners. Each partner must be able to identify how they will benefit from the alliance. Management should ask the following questions when considering an alliance:

1. What is the benefit to the businesses that will be involved?

2. Will customers be accepting of the new venture?

3. Are staff able to work with the staff of the other businesses? Is there a rivalry that could cause conflict?

4. Is the management of the potential partners adequately committed, experienced and skilled?

Because a strategic alliance involves complex arrangements and investments it is very important to plan and negotiate terms of the alliance. Some of the issues that need to be resolved are:

- Set clear goals for the alliance.

- Document the resources to be provided by each partner.

- Identify the key performance indicators that the alliance must achieve for it to be worthwhile.

- Detail the type of alliance to be formed.

- List operating issues that need to be addressed to achieve the results.

- Consider the need to protect your company's intellectual property before entering an alliance: who will own the intellectual property developed in the alliance?

CHAPTER 8
Export risk

'In a world that changing really quickly, the only strategy
that is guaranteed to fail is not taking risks.'
– Mark Zuckerberg –

In a global economy businesses deal with suppliers and customers around the world. International business depends upon secure and reliable transportation for goods. Just as important is the secure and reliable transfer of money. Entering into contracts and business relationships is more likely if the people involved can be sure their money will be safely transferred.

When dealing with customers domestically it is easier to gather information about their credit rating and to communicate with them to solve problems. It is difficult to do this with international customers, making international transactions riskier.

RISKS INVOLVED IN INTERNATIONAL TRANSACTIONS

Risks involved in international transactions include:

* delays in payment or non-payment
* loss or damage in transit
* loss due to exchange rate variations
* increased transportation costs.

The best way to reduce financial risk when exporting is to arrange prepayment of invoices. A customer signs a sales contract and makes payment up front. The Australian business receives the money so there is no risk of non-payment later on. The exporter could require customers to pay the full price or a large deposit.

Australian banks offer international money transfers. Electronic payments are sent from a branch or via Internet banking from Australia to banks in other countries. You need the bank account details of the business overseas or provide them with your bank details if they are paying you. Electronic transfers can take from hours to days to arrive. Transfers may be delayed due to time zone differences.

Some financial institutions provide a foreign currency account for businesses that have transactions in foreign currency regularly. Rather than having to convert payments and receipts to Australian dollars every time, an account balance is held in a foreign currency. If a business deals with suppliers or customers in the US, for example, it would maintain a bank account in US dollars. There are also documents that can be used to manage the risks involved in international transactions.

Non-payment of monies

A financial risk is not receiving payment from the customer after incurring costs and possibly providing the goods or service. Unlike a domestic transaction, it may be very difficult to track down a customer that hasn't paid in another country and difficult to find legal recourse to recover the debt.

It can take longer to get paid for exports than for sales to domestic customers. You may not be paid in full until the products or services have been delivered. Transporting goods to other countries can be slow; there may be weeks between dispatch and delivery.

The longer the delay between providing the goods or service and payment, the higher the risk of non-payment. This has an impact on cash flow.

Prepayment is a way to reduce the risk of non-payment. This is when the customer or client overseas agrees to pay in advance of receiving the goods or service. While it is commonly used for online sales, there is generally resistance to prepayment because the customer has the risk of non-delivery and an adverse impact on cash flow because of up front payments.

Prepayment may be made by:

- transfer through a bank
- credit card payment
- international bank cheque or bank draft.

The documentation explored below outlines ways to manage the risk of non-payment.

Documentation to manage risk

There are a number of documents that can be used to manage the risks involved in international transactions.

Documentary letter of credit

Before an exporter sends goods overseas they need to be sure that the customer will pay for them. Documentary credit is a form of guarantee from the customer's bank that the money will be paid. The letter of credit will detail terms that must be met before payment is made.

Terms could include that the goods arrive as ordered, without damage and within a certain time. If these terms are met the bank will transfer the money to the exporter's bank. If the customer does not have the funds in their account their bank will make the payment to the exporter then chase the customer for reimbursement.

YouTube
Letter of credit

Documents against payment

An exporter receives an order from a customer. Goods are manufactured or sourced as per the order. The exporter uses their bank to send a bill and any documents that will allow the buyer to collect the goods to the customer's bank.

The customer's bank will give the documents to the buyer only after payment is made. The customer makes the payment to their bank and it is forwarded to exporter's bank.

Insurance

A way to encourage people to buy goods is to offer generous credit terms. Credit terms overcome the obstacle of the customer not having the funds to pay for the goods. But there is a risk to exporters when they give credit to customers. It is the same risk that businesses face when selling goods domestically but it is more difficult to chase payments when you're dealing with customers in other countries. Three types of insurance in exporting are:

EXPORT CREDIT INSURANCE	POLITICAL RISKS INSURANCE	TRANSIT OR SHIPPING INSURANCE
Export credit insurance is a way exporters prepare for possible bad debts. For example, an Australian company sells goods to a company in China on credit. Before payment is made the Chinese importer is declared insolvent and unable to pay its debts. If the exporter has export credit insurance the insurance company will pay the business what is owed.	If an Australian exporter is selling goods to customers in countries that have civil unrest or wars, they can insure against non-payment and loss or damage to goods. Political risks insurance also covers damage to an exporter's business due to changes in laws and regulations and other government restrictions in the country of the customer; for example, if civil unrest makes it impossible to transport goods or the government freezes all international transactions.	Businesses undertaking international transactions can also use transit or shipping insurance to mitigate unexpected losses. Transit or shipping insurance covers the goods while they are being delivered. If they are lost or damaged the business is able to make a claim.

Hedging

The uncertainty of the Australian dollar against other currencies has an impact on the profit of Australian businesses. If a business deals with international customers and suppliers, managing foreign exchange variations is a daily issue. Currency fluctuation is a financial risk for international business and may be managed through hedging.

If payment is to be received in foreign currency, movements in exchange rates can adversely affect the amount of money received and reduce the profit margin.

A currency exchange rate is the price at which one currency is exchanged for another currency at one point in time. If a business deals with international customers and suppliers on a regular basis they are at risk because of exchange rate variations that do not go in their favour.

A risk for exporters is if currency exchange rates change in the time between signing the contract and the customer making the payment. For example, an Australian business signs a sales contract with a US customer for USD10 000. At the time of the contract signing the exchange rate is USD1.00 to AUD1.10. This means that at the time the contract was signed the Australian business would receive:

USD10 000 x 1.10 = AUD11 000

A few weeks have passed and the US customer is now making payment. At the time of payment the exchange rate is $1.00USD to $1.06AUD. This means that when the customer pays the invoice the Australian business will receive:

USD10 000 x 1.06 = AUD10 600

The business has lost a cash inflow of $400 through a fall in the exchange rate.

The best way to protect against exchange rate losses is to require customers to pay in your currency. Exchange rate variations have no impact on the income and there is no delay or fees associated with converting payments in foreign currencies. Or the contract could be signed with a set exchange rate, the rate at the time of signing the contract, for example.

Another way is to hedge against the risk. Hedging is a method to reduce losses from exchange rate variations. The basic idea of hedging is to make an investment that makes a return that can be used to offset any losses from another investment. Exporters would hedge against unfavourable changes in exchange rates.

Forward	Option
The exporter and the customer sign a contract that sets an exchange rate for the transaction.	An exchange rate is set which can be used instead of the current exchange rate at the time of payment.
When payment is made the agreed exchange rate will apply.	If the current exchange rate is better for the business it can be used in the transaction instead of the agreed rate.

HEDGING

Figure 8.1: Two forms of hedges are forwards and options:

Another way to manage currency exchange risk is to list goods and services and quote work in Australian dollars. The price will stay constant despite changes in exchange rates.

CHAPTER 9
Business innovation

'For good ideas and true innovation, you need human interaction, conflict, argument, debate.'
– Margaret Heffernan –

INNOVATION

Innovation is about creating something new, and improving existing systems, products and processes. It can be a radical change or change built from incremental improvements. An outcome of innovation is the continuous improvement of products, processes and systems. This involves building on good practice and identifying ways to keep getting better.

Innovation can lead to:

- improved economic outcomes
- survival and growth
- increased employment
- increased exports
- improved skills in the workforce
- new ways of working such as virtual work groups
- better management of environmental impact.Ideas for innovation come from analysing business information and data such as that shown here in the diagram.

Continuous improvement and innovation has long been a part of business operations management. The role of innovation is also applied to the products and services a business offers to create and maintain competitive advantage. Process innovation can increase safety, reduce costs and increase profit by improving quality, efficiency and reducing waste.

Innovation can be based around process and/or product.

YouTube
The Explainer: Disruptive innovation

SOURCES OF IDEAS FOR INNOVATION

Customer motivations and preferences

Feedback from customers

Competitor analysis

Sales and cost data

Feedback and ideas from staff

Feedback from suppliers

Market research

Production and quality data

Process innovation

Process innovation is about changing and improving how a business operates and/or manufactures, distributes and markets its products and services. An emerging process innovation is cloud computing. Companies are using it to increase efficiency and reduce costs.

CASE STUDY

Australian company, Moraitis Fresh, supplies supermarkets, fruit markets and national restaurant chains with fresh fruits and vegetables. Moraitis placed radio frequency identification tags on tomato trays to track the origin, packing date, type, quality and size of the tons of tomatoes it ships every day. This means that it can track the precise amount and quality of tomatoes in its supply chain at any point in time. The company can respond rapidly to customer requests for a specific volume and grade of tomato and tell its customers exactly when and where the produce was grown, packed and shipped. This real-time data also improves financial control, allowing Moraitis to pay growers based on the actual quality and number of tomatoes received.

Product innovation

Product innovation refers to changing and improving the features, materials or functions of a product or service.

Nintendo

Nintendo Wii changed the way games are played by innovating controller technology. Nintendo introduced a hand-held device that translates movement into visual screen feedback. This has introduced gaming to a new market and created a niche for Nintendo.

Dyson

Dyson are well known for their product innovations in how their appliances work. For example, the cyclonic vacuum, the bladeless fan and the 'Airblade' hand dryer. Dyson prevent competitors from copying their products and taking market share by using a range of intellectual property protections including patents, registered designs, trademarks and copyright.

The benefits of innovation

A business case can be made for innovation. Before implementing a change its cost and benefits must be analysed to ensure that it will have a positive impact on the business.

Benefits of innovation include the following.

Financial gain

Innovation may lead to increased income or a new income source through the creation of a new market or the capture of more market share. Innovation may also prolong a product's life cycle by delaying the onset of the decline stage. By adding features or improving quality and performance, customer demand can be maintained or increased. This will prolong the maturity stage of the product life cycle or result in a period of sales growth.

Process innovation may reduce waste and costs which also results in sustained profit. Innovation may involve a less expensive manufacturing process or substituting materials for higher quality options which decreases defects and production losses.

Apple have perfected this approach by offering incremental improvements to existing products to drive sales growth. For example, each iteration of the iPhone is marginally different to the last but results in high global demand from consumers upgrading to the 'new' product.

Expansion of global market presence

An innovation can be marketed to the world if the intellectual property driving it is protected. The competitive advantage created by the innovation can be translated into global competitiveness.

The innovation could lead to options for expansion such as franchising and licensing. Technologies such as e-commerce, groupware and online ordering, distribution and payment systems make global expansion possible.

Process innovations may reduce costs and increase production capacity. These will enable a business to implement marketing strategies to enter or expand global markets.

Increased market share

Innovation may result in a new product or service that captures market share or creates a new market. Product innovation may create a fad, respond to existing customer demand in a new and better way or anticipate a market trend. Process innovation may result in a better way to interact with customers, such as social media, online purchasing and payment methods.

A company can enhance their public image and potentially consumer demand and loyalty through environmental management innovation. If a company uses new or improved technology to reduce the carbon footprint, reduce waste or better manage pollution they can promote their commitment to sustainability and being 'green'. This will increase consumer awareness of the brand and may result in a competitive advantage over similar products and services that may not be as environmentally friendly.

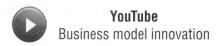

YouTube
Business model innovation

Factors that affect innovation success

What is 'success' in innovation? How do you know when an innovation is successful? Some indicators of successful innovations are:

- **It works:** the innovation has got to the stage where it is fully developed, it works and it can be taken to the next stage of commercialisation and market launch.

- **Commercialisation:** an innovation has been developed into a product or service and packaged with marketing strategies and launched into the market.

- **Integration into a product or service:** the innovation has been incorporated into existing products or services, eg. improved quality, added features, better performance.

- **Income:** sales and revenue can be attributed to the innovation.

Timing

Innovation is more likely to succeed during times of prosperity than times of economic slowing or downturn. Consumers are more likely to try a new product or service if they have more discretionary income and consumer confidence is good. If there is potential demand for a new product or service, retailers and wholesalers are more likely to take it on because of the lower risk.

In stronger economic times a company is more likely to take on the risk of dedicating time, money and focus to creating something new.

The stage if the product life cycle will also have an impact on the success of an innovation. When a product is in the growth or maturity stage there is already brand awareness and a market presence. Consumers know about the product, many have bought it and there are established distribution and marketing strategies.

An innovation can build on existing success and exploit the market share and marketing systems that already exist. A company will also have substantial data from market research and their customer database to refine innovations and generate ideas. At the maturity stage the company may also have made profits that could finance innovation.

Market research is largely based on the past. It identifies preferences, data and characteristics on a past point in time. Ideas may also be based on current capabilities and performance of the company. Things may change. There may be changes in the economy, consumer behavior, staff turnover, technology and other factors that may have an impact on the nature and viability of the innovation.

Management needs to use their judgement and the information at hand to identify the ways the company and the business environment may change, to anticipate change. That way they can manage the risk of innovation and prepare for the future.

Cost

Innovation is risky and it usually requires considerable investment of time and money either from retained profits or from external funding such as loans, grants, share issues. An innovation may take some time to be commercialised and profitable (if at all). In the meantime, the company must bear the increased operational costs.

An important responsibility is to know when to pull the plug on an innovation. Sunken cost describes the money and effort already committed to an innovation. Regardless of the money and effort already spent, if the project is no longer beneficial or cost-effective, the costs that have been sunk into the innovation cannot be recovered and it should be terminated.

This has been identified as an 'innovation death spiral'. Financing innovation allocates people and money to a project and takes resources away from existing operations. If an innovation looks like it will be unsuccessful, a company may allocate more people and money to the project to try and make it work. This puts greater pressure on the core business and decreases the resources available for operating and marketing existing products and services. The losses from the innovation project can have an impact on the company as a whole and jeopardise its survival. This may also happen if a company invests substantial resources into incremental innovation, making small changes to existing products with little impact on the market.

One way to assess an innovation is in terms of net cash flow – earn versus burn: the difference between the income from the innovation (earn) and the money spent to make it happen (burn).

Marketing strategy

To successfully commercialise an innovation, a company must align production and marketing strategies. A radical change may require an education campaign to build understanding about the need for the innovation and the benefits it will bring to consumers.

Marketing strategy may need a range of approaches including public relations, advertising, and changes to packaging and promotion within distribution networks. These will build awareness, interest and desire for the innovation. Wholesalers and retailers will need to be educated so they can sell the features and benefits to the consumer to help generate demand.

Positioning may also have an impact on the success of innovations. If a company has built an image and reputation for being innovative and high quality, consumers, wholesalers and retailers are more likely to believe their claims about new and improved products and services.

Technology

Technological discovery or invention can provide the stimulus for innovation. A new technology may enable a company to do something they could not and give them the platform to change their business. An example is the way that secure online payment systems and a stable Internet allows companies to change to digital distribution of products and services.

Technology development can lead to radical and disruptive innovations; not only in the area of computing and software. Other technologies such as nanotechnology and genetic modification have created new markets and new products and services.

How a company manages technology will also have an impact on the success of innovation. Management needs a strategic outlook for technology and the expertise to manage the innovation process.

Managers must be able to:

- **manage and analyse information:** market research, customer databases, identify trends and opportunities

- **generate ideas:** facilitate meetings, support a creative workplace, learn from mistakes, short list options

- **realise ideas:** be able to turn an idea or a concept into a reality, drive the process and keep people focused and within budget

- **protect the technology:** understand intellectual property and know how to protect it.

Intellectual property protection

A company is more likely to benefit from an innovation if they can prevent competitors from using it too. An innovative product design, manufacturing technology or improvements made to features or packaging may result in increased sales, a new market or increased profit through lower costs.

Protecting the design through a patent, copyright or a registered design will stop competitors from making and launching their own versions and benefiting from the time and money another company invested in the innovation.

CASE STUDY

Lego had been in a decline in sales and profits since the 1990s. To turn it around they invested heavily in innovation to create a range of new products including virtual Lego and toys that moved away from their core business of construction. One of their experiments was called Galidor. It was a buildable action figure and also a huge, expensive failure. Galidor had electronics in it that you could play games with, an accompanying video game and a TV show.

Lego did what you are supposed to do when facing a challenge, thought outside the box. They changed the way they did business, started marketing strategies they had no expertise in and launched stand-alone products very different to everything else they sold.

Some innovations were successful (Bionicle, Harry Potter and Star Wars-themed Lego) but the costs of the unsuccessful innovations (Technic, Galidor, Lego Baby) almost led to disaster.

CHAPTER 10
Unit 3 Management activities

'Despite different cultures, middle-class youth all over the world seem to live their lives as if in a parallel universe. They get up in the morning, put on their Levi's and Nikes, grab their caps and backpacks, and Sony personal CD players and head for school.'
– Naomi Klein (1999) –

Topic study

1. What are the two options for entering an overseas market?
2. Describe two benefits of a global brand.
3. What are two things included in a feasibility study?
4. What is the difference between primary and secondary data?
5. What are two approaches to adapting strategies for international markets?
6. List three advantages of strategic alliances.
7. What are two disadvantages of strategic alliances?
8. What is a hostile acquisition?
9. What is a merger?
10. What is a joint venture?
11. List two risks in international transactions.
12. Explain one type of insurance used in international transactions.
13. What is hedging?
14. What are two forms of hedging?
15. What documentation is used to manage international transaction risks?
16. What are two things innovation can lead to?
17. What is process innovation?
18. What is product innovation?
19. List two benefits of innovation.
20. What are two factors that have an impact on the success of innovations?

Business research

1. Global strategic alliances

i.   Explain the difference between merger and joint venture.

ii. What are the advantages and disadvantages of both forms of strategic alliance?

iii. Suggest a possible merger and joint venture involving Australian and international companies.

iv. Find examples of what could be considered as a 'bear hug' acquisition.

2. Standardisation and adaptation

i.   Compare standardisation and adaptation in global marketing strategies.

ii. What are the advantages and disadvantages of both?

iii. Include examples of companies and products that have standardised their strategies and examples of those that have adapted them.

3. Innovation

Prepare a written report on how a company could encourage innovation in the workplace. Explain four strategies that a company could use to create an innovative workplace culture and encourage their employees to innovate. Use the 4 Plan to organise your research.

4. Global growth

Conduct a Force Field Analysis to analyse global growth from the perspective of an Australian company. Look at the benefits and the challenges for an Australian company to expand into international markets. Make a recommendation based on your analysis.

Response

1. Innovation

i.   What is the difference between incremental and disruptive innovation? Give examples of both.

ii. Use products you know and suggest incremental and disruptive innovations.

2. Innovation

Research each of the following technologies. Describe what they are and if they represent incremental or disruptive innovation. Explain what form of innovation they are – process or product or both?

• Apple watch

• Lithography method for microchips

• Virtual reality headsets

- Pilkington glass method
- Google Glass part deux
- The electrifying wheel
- Barcodes and scanners on inventory
- All-in-one blood testing device

Produce a slideshow to present your research findings and discussion of the forms of innovation.

3. Global strategic alliances

Cadbury Schweppes was taken over by Kraft foods in 2010. Immediately following the takeover five of Cadbury's senior executives quit the company. Prior to the takeover Kraft promised that there would be no major changes to the operations of Cadbury.

After the takeover Kraft closed a factory with the loss of 500 jobs and some of the senior jobs were moved from the UK to Zurich to reduce corporation tax. This meant staff had to relocate or leave.

In March 2012 Kraft announced that the takeover had been a big success: 'We have gone through this consolidation process and the business has continued to perform really well. Our business in the UK grew by 4% – it goes from strength to strength'.

i.   Acquisitions and mergers may have problems that can have an impact on their success. Describe two difficulties and how they can be managed to increase the likelihood of success.

ii. Profit at Cadbury's increased by 4% during a period of limited growth. Explain how acquisitions and mergers can have a beneficial effect on the performance of the business involved.

iii. What disadvantages could there be of acquisitions and mergers to the economy and community?

iv. Should there be a role for governments in acquisitions and mergers or should the market decide what happens?

Consider the following acquisitions and mergers and identify what type of merger was involved:

Activity	Type
A national newspaper buys a paper mill in Malaysia	
A small printing firm in Perth goes into partnership with a similar business in Bunbury	
A furniture manufacturer buys a chain of furniture stores	
A large insurance company buys a shipbuilding company and an energy company	
A computer software developer takes over an Internet service provider	

Choose two examples above and explain the benefits of the move to the business.

4. Export risk – Hedging

Hedging can be likened to an insurance policy that limits the impact of foreign exchange risk and can be used by global businesses.

i.   Explain how Exchange Traded Funds (ETFs) can be used to mitigate foreign exchange risk.

ii.   Find examples of services financial institutions offer to manage the risk of currency fluctuations.

iii. Consider an Australian business that manufactures products using imported components from Asia. They sell their products in Europe. Describe how currency fluctuations could have an impact on the business.

5. Global strategic alliances

A firm must decide whether to make a component part in-house, or to contract it out to an independent supplier. Manufacturing the part requires a non-recoverable investment in specialised assets. The most efficient suppliers are located in countries with currencies that many foreign exchange analysts expect to appreciate substantially over the next decade.

What are the pros and cons of:

i.   Manufacturing the component in-house?
ii.   Outsourcing manufacture to an independent supplier?

Discuss which option you would recommend.

CHAPTER 11
Change for success

'The price of doing the same old thing is far
higher than the price of change.'
– Bill Clinton –

CHANGE MANAGEMENT

Change management is a process that coordinates business systems to control and manage change within an organisation. Businesses operate in an environment that is always changing. Change in the business environment is brought about by new government policies and laws, demographic changes, developments in technology and increased competition.

What worked in the past may not work now. Management and directors may decide to respond to change through a strategic process of creating a new vision and new goals implemented through new business structures and systems.

There are two important aspects of change management: the business and the people. A successful change relies on success in both aspects.

- **The business:** requires successful implementation of new systems, policies and technologies to respond to the business environment and new strategic direction.

- **The people:** all employees must understand the reason why the business must change and the purpose of the change process. Management must be clear about any repercussions for staff (promotions, demotions, redundancies) and the role of staff in the change process. Change will succeed if employees are supportive and motivated to change.

Change can take many forms and must be managed if it has an impact on the business. Examples of changes include:

- new products and services
- sacking people to cut costs
- outsourcing
- starting business online
- entry into a strategic alliance
- significant change in laws and regulations
- international expansion

- a move into franchising
- buying and selling businesses.

These changes have an impact on everything a business does and involve changes to procedures, policies, how staff do their jobs, how to use new technology and equipment, and where people work.

Factors that increase the likelihood of a successful change process are shown here.

Businesses are not stagnant, they are dynamic and change is always occurring in them. In order to have continuous improvement, a business will have to monitor and modify its operations. The business environment is also dynamic and to keep up with changes, a business will have to adapt its mode of operations. Not all stakeholders will be happy with change for various reasons and may resist any attempt to modify processes and procedures.

CRITICAL SUCCESS FACTORS

- Be clear about the purpose of change
- Set goals and a timeline for change
- Write and change plan
- Identify risks and threats to change
- Communicate frequently with staff
- Sell the benefits of change to stakeholders
- Develop change agent skills or hire a change agent
- Define the roles of staff in the process

Some changes in the business environment include the introduction of the carbon tax, the rise of videoconferencing, changes in work, health and safety laws, paid parental leave, environmental regulations and superannuation.

Employees may resist change because they feel that they may lose career opportunities, may lose their skills or may even lose their jobs. They may worry about new training that is required. Change may mean that the workplace is reorganised, which places employees outside their comfort zone and may lead to low morale.

Owners may also resist change because they may have concerns about the costs involved, such as the purchase of new equipment and redundancy payments made to staff who are losing jobs. These costs will reduce the return on the investment they have made in making the changes.

Managers will resist change if they feel overburdened with responsibility. They sometimes feel inertia (or lack of motivation or energy) toward the change with a feeling of 'if it isn't broken, don't fix it'.

Change can be viewed as a positive. For example, employees can often gain inspiration and develop new skills and promotion prospects by retraining and purchasing new equipment or reorganising the workplace can improve efficiency.

To overcome resistance to change, it is important that management consider:

- why the change is occurring
- a sound rationale for the change
- the most strategic time to make the change.

Management must ensure that all stakeholders are included in the planning and discussion of change. By consulting employees and involving them in decisions they can feel a sense of ownership and control over the direction of change. In this way, managers can gain support for the change rather than encounter resistance.

Resistance to change

Resistance to change is when employees oppose or struggle to accept changes in the workplace.

Resistance to change may be expressed as criticism, nitpicking details, failure to adopt new policies and procedures, sarcasm, missed training and meetings, arguments with management and co-workers and, at the extreme, workplace sabotage.

Employees may be resistant to change if they feel that the changes are being implemented without consultation, enough explanation or without the support of management. Employees may resist because the change involves an increased workload or the possibility of losing authority or their job. It is also very stressful to have to learn new skills, work with new people and adapt to new routines.

Financial costs

A change may be so significant that it involves rebuilding the whole business, in which case the financial cost will be great. On the other hand, incremental change may be involved, where changes can be more easily budgeted for. The projected cost of implementing change may cause resistance, particularly if the benefits of the change are uncertain or unclear.

Purchasing new materials and equipment

New technologies, manufacturing processes or new point of sale technology is costly to purchase and install. Costs may include new stationery, uniforms and rebadging vehicles if there is a change in corporate identification (logo, corporate colours, slogan). A change in a product, service or marketing strategy may mean that advertising campaigns will have to be replaced, and in-store displays changed as well as product brochures, manuals and websites.

Redundancy payouts

Workplace change may involve closing down or outsourcing functions, combining jobs, or projects ending. These will lead to jobs no longer being required. Employees who are made redundant will need to be paid their financial entitlements. Redundancy costs will have an impact on the profitability of the change.

Retraining

Any significant change requires staff to learn new skills. There are costs involved in providing the training, and lost productivity while staff are attending training.

Inertia of managers and owners

In physics, inertia is the tendency of a body to preserve its state of rest or uniform motion unless acted upon by an external force. In business, inertia is about being stuck in a routine because it has worked in the past. Inertia is the lack of motivation to do something about a problem and the preference to continue with the status quo.

Managers may display inertia because they:

- do not want to deal with the problem
- may not have the skills to solve the problem
- see that it is safer to keep what they know rather than risking the change.

"What if we don't change anything at all ... and something magical just happens."

To break inertia and motivate people to change:

1. Create dissatisfaction

Make the case for change, convince employees that there are problems with the way things are done currently, the change will fix the problems and there will be benefits to them and the business.

2. Involve people

Involve the people who need to implement the change in its planning. If they understand the change and how it will work they are more likely to be committed to it. Get their ideas and feedback and find ways to resolve resistance along the way.

3. Share the plan

Ensure that employees know what is happening and have clear goals. People will be able to understand the steps of the change, anticipate what will happen, and uncertainty and fear will be reduced.

Cultural incompatibility in mergers/takeovers

Mergers or takeovers result in two businesses, each with its own strong culture, becoming one. Staff will have different approaches to doing their work. New work groups are required and friendships are broken. Therefore staff resist adjustments in their jobs. When they are forced to do so, motivation for change falls.

This is also true of cultural differences in a global business. Cultural differences can create barriers to effective communication, the growth of working relationships, and building a common understanding of the company.

YouTube
Overcoming resistance to change – isn't it obvious?

Staff attitude

Staff may feel that they do not have the skills to learn new systems and processes. They may resist because of their fear of failure. Staff must be supported, there must be training and education to support the change and there must be a realistic time frame to implement the change. It is also a good idea to acknowledge how difficult the change is and to celebrate successes along the way.

Staff may feel overwhelmed or powerless when faced with major changes in the workplace. Some employees may embrace them and others may remember bad experiences in the past. Past experiences of workplace change that was managed badly may result in staff feeling pessimistic, cheated or critical.

Another aspect is a person's tolerance for risk or uncertainty. People with a high tolerance for uncertainty may have the attitude of change being a challenge, an opportunity to learn something new or just part of life. Others with a low tolerance will experience fear, stress and worry about something replacing the routines of the past.

Staff's attitude towards the company and management will also have an impact on the success of a change. If employees trust managers and have a good working relationship they are more likely to commit to the change and forgive mistakes and setbacks. If there is an attitude of mistrust, if employees do not believe that the management can succeed, then the change is doomed to failure.

Ripple effects

Like tossing a rock into a pond, change creates ripples throughout a workplace. The ripples disrupt other departments, suppliers and customers, and they may resist the change. Change can affect people and systems in ways that were not anticipated. Leaders should enlarge the circle of stakeholders. They must consider all affected parties, however indirect, and work with them to make change successful and long-lasting.

Loss of control

Change interferes with autonomy and can make people feel that they've lost control over their territory. It's not just political, as in who has the power. Our sense of self-determination is often the first thing to go when faced with a potential change coming from someone else. Smart leaders leave room for those affected by change to make choices. They invite others into the planning, giving them ownership.

Poor timing

Change must be introduced when there are no other major initiatives going on and not at a busy time of the year. Undue resistance can occur because changes are introduced in an insensitive manner or at an awkward time.

Resistance to change may not always be a negative. Some managers and workers may have an instinct about something that may not work based on their experience and knowledge of the workplace and industry. The resistance may also mean that options and procedures are questioned, examined and improved.

Preparing people for change

For change to be successful, employees must be prepared for it. This is a common criticism of politicians that do not 'sell' their policies. The change may be valid but people must understand the need for change and the benefits of the proposed change. It is also more than just having a plan. A good plan isn't enough to motivate people to change if they do not understand the need and benefits of it.

Change is more likely to be successful if you do the following:

- **Prepare for change:** consult, research, plan, discuss options.
- **Communicate the change:** the need for change, what is planned and the benefits it will bring.
- **Ensure involvement:** consult all stakeholders, consult the staff affected, gather feedback about the plan and incorporate it.
- **Provide support:** information, training, letting staff vent their fears and frustrations.
- **Show leadership:** role model the new processes and strategies, motivate people by having a clear vision for the change.

Lewin's stages of change

Kurt Lewin identified three stages of change that an organisation goes through. Each stage must succeed if a change is to be successful.

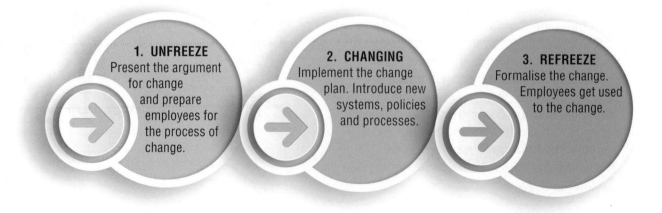

1. UNFREEZE Present the argument for change and prepare employees for the process of change.

2. CHANGING Implement the change plan. Introduce new systems, policies and processes.

3. REFREEZE Formalise the change. Employees get used to the change.

1. Unfreeze

It is understandable that people who have worked in a job feel comfortable and have a sense of identity linked to the work they do. If they find out that jobs, processes and work culture is changing they can feel anxious about their future. Unfreezing is a process to help people feel comfortable about being 'unstuck', freeing themselves from the old and embracing the vision of the new. Like ice, ideas and expectations can be hard to move until they unfreeze and become fluid.

Unfreezing occurs through communicating the purpose of the change, having a clear plan and being open and honest about the role of employees and the impact on their working life. The change team and management must convince employees that there are costs and risks of not changing and benefits and opportunities created by change.

"It's good to see at least one employee who has overcome her resistance to change."

This stage involves leadership, staff meetings, small group workshops and the distribution of information verbally, in writing and by email. Employee feedback is sought so concerns can be resolved.

2. Changing

The change plan is implemented and new policies, systems and processes are introduced, for example a new computer network, new employee incentives or bringing in staff from a merger or acquisition. Communication is vital as well as linking employee rewards and recognition to the new ways of doing business.

3. Refreeze

This stage is about formalising the new policies, systems and processes. It may take time for employees to become comfortable with the new ways of doing their jobs and to learn new routines and processes. Management needs to keep communicating, celebrating successes and rewarding commitment to the new organisation to keep people motivated and committed.

 YouTube
Lewin: Stage model of change – unfreezing, changing, refreezing

Change management can be unsuccessful. There may be resistance to change because employees fear they will lose their jobs or authority. They may not be convinced that change is necessary.

The main factors of unsuccessful change are:

- poor planning
- lack of skills and experience of the change team
- poor leadership by the change agents
- lack of communication throughout the process
- lack of coordination among managers.

Successful change depends on all employees believing in the goals and being committed to building a new organisation. Without frequent communication, good leadership and a clear plan, employees will not feel confident about the change.

Lewin's Force Field Analysis

For change management to be successful employees must be convinced that the forces for change are stronger than the forces against change. Force field analysis is a method to analyse and compare the forces of change. It is a tool that can be used as part of the unfreezing stage to help employees understand the need for change.

To organise thinking a template is used. In a meeting or in brainstorming sessions the template is used to records forces that support change and those that create resistance and obstacles to change. The nominal technique is used in the analysis. Ideas for forces are brainstormed and recorded. Then the forces are reviewed and the most important kept and rated according to their importance. The rating could be out of 5 or 10, the higher the rating the more impact the force has on the proposed change.

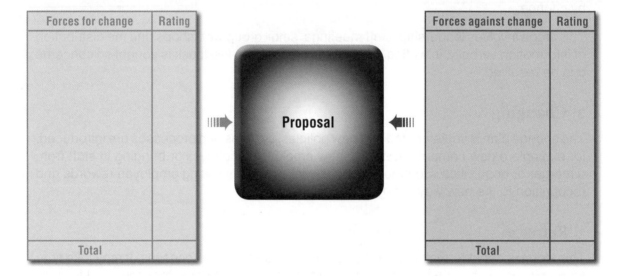

A proposal looks viable if the force for change score is higher than the force against change score. The analysis lists the forces that can be supported and built on and the forces against change that can be managed and reduced. If the forces against change result is greater, the management may be able to find ways to reduce the forces and the total. For example, communication across countries may be a force against change. If a company is able to introduce videoconferencing or groupware then the rating for that force is reduced.

The analysis also assists management to develop action plans that exploit the forces for change and reduce the forces against change.

YouTube
Using the Force Field Analysis

Kotter's 8 Steps

John Kotter developed eight steps for change management to make change more likely to be successful and a long term change. He saw these eight steps (see below) to be critical success factors in managing change.

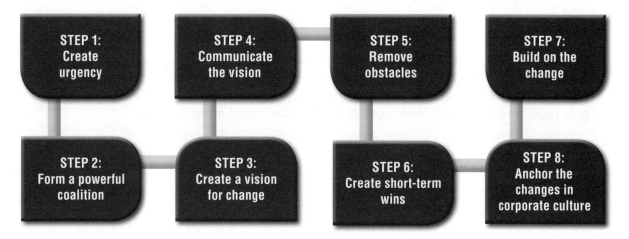

❶ Step 1: Create urgency

People will be motivated for change if they understand why they should do it and the costs or risks if they don't change. Communicate the problems and reasons for change and get people talking about it, sharing ideas. Kotter suggests that 75% of management must support change to be successful. They must be convinced that change is necessary.

How to do it:

- Identify threats and opportunities in the business environment.
- Discuss the reasons for change to get people talking and thinking.
- Ask for input and support from staff.

❷ Step 2: Form a powerful coalition

With management on side they will work to make changes. Identify people with leadership and technical skills that can be relied on to make the change happen. Convince people that change is necessary.

How to do it:

- Identify leaders in the workplace.
- Create a change team that will work together to make it happen.
- Have a good mix of people from different departments and different levels.

❸ Step 3: Create a vision for change

Develop a clear goal for change so people know what they are working towards. They will see the benefit and why the work and stress is worthwhile. What people have to do will make more sense if they see what the business is trying to achieve.

How to do it:

- Use the change team to develop a goal.
- Write a clear plan for the change process to achieve the goal.
- Ensure the vision is easy to understand and communicate to others.

❹ Step 4: Communicate the vision

One staff meeting announcing the change is not enough. People throughout the workplace and work sites must understand what is happening. Good and regular communication is important to deal with fears and concerns about change. Hold meetings, talk to individuals, give regular updates and seek feedback about how the change is going.

How to do it:

- Talk often about the change vision.
- Seek feedback and address concerns.
- Lead by example.

❺ Step 5: Remove obstacles

Planning for change includes anticipating what could go wrong or delay success. Put things in place to address these issues and use feedback to identify other barriers to success. Obstacles blocking change and how to remove them are summarised in Table 11.1 below.

Table 11.1: Obstacles to change

Obstacle	How to remove it
Lack of skill and expertise	Bring in consultants and experts to train staff and assist with the change process, research and learn from what similar businesses have done and how to avoid their mistakes, consult staff and draw on their experience and skills
Fear of change	Communicate the vision and goals, discuss why the change is needed and what the risks are with the status quo, include people in making decisions and seek feedback and ideas, keep people informed about progress
Location of staff	Use technology, emails, newsletters, team and staff meetings and site visits to include all staff, include people from all work areas in the change team

How to do it:

- Use meetings and communication to identify barriers and find solutions.
- Reward people for making change happen.
- Identify people who are resisting change and try to convince them of its importance.

❻ Step 6: Create short-term wins

The change plan should have short-term targets. People will be more motivated if they can see progress being made and targets are celebrated and their efforts are recognised.

How to do it:

- Take care when choosing early targets, failure to achieve them will jeopardise future success and commitment.
- Communicate successes to all staff.

❼ Step 7: Build on the change

Long-term success depends on changing how work is done but more importantly the workplace culture. Change involves learning new ways and believing they are better thanthe old methods. If people don't believe that, the change won't last.

How to do it:

- Keep reviewing and improving to make sure the change is working.
- Ensure all policies, procedures, manuals and instructions are updated.
- Seek feedback from staff.
- Identify where the new methods are not being followed.

❽ Step 8: Anchor the changes in corporate culture

Ensure workplace leaders, teams and new staff continue to support the change. Ensure that business strategies and goals are aligned with the change.

How to do it:

- Keep celebrating successes.
- Show how success has come from change.
- Keep workplace leaders informed so they can answer questions from their work teams.

YouTube
Explaining Kotter's 8 Step Change Model

CHAPTER 12
Managing diversity

'Strength lies in differences, not in similarities.'
– Stephen R Covey –

MANAGING DIVERSITY

Diversity refers to the range of traits a group of people have: gender, age, language, ethnicity, cultural background, disability, sexual orientation or religious belief. Diversity also includes the many differences people have in educational level, skill level, socio-economic background, personality, geographic location and family situation.

Our diverse Australian society is reflected in the diversity in our workplaces as shown here.

Managing diversity in a workplace allows a business to draw on the largest pool of potential employees and it provides the widest possible range of talents, skills and ideas. Diversity can improve morale and loyalty and can lower the level of staff turnover.

People feel valued, welcomed and supported if their abilities are recognised and ideas listened to. Because diverse workforces have people with a wide range of experiences, ideas, skills and perspectives there is the potential for higher levels of creativity and innovation.

If businesses are going to sell products and services around the world, they need a mix of employees with varied perspectives and experiences. They will need staff who understand different countries and cultures, who can work around the world and who understand the markets they are working in. A diverse workforce can better understand and cater to the diverse community around it.

Managing diversity involves designing flexible ways to work. People with disabilities or with family commitments could work from home or on a part time roster. People who need to work part-time may benefit from a job share arrangement.

Older workers may need to phase down their hours over time. These methods and others aim to make sure that those who want to participate in the workplace can, so they and the business benefit.

Managing diversity is about treating people as individuals and building a workplace that recognises the value of good relationships and a strong work ethic. It can also mean that a business can retain staff who have valuable skills and experience. Instead of someone resigning because of a change in their life, different working arrangements could be used to enable them to keep working while considering their needs.

To manage diversity, businesses must have an internal culture, procedures, practices and workplace environments to recruit, retain and reward people with disabilities, people from a wide range of cultures and languages, both men and women, and workers that are young and old.

Practical measures are necessary to cater for diversity. Ramps, wider doorways, automatic doors and office layouts can be used to cater for people in wheelchairs.

When working in a diverse and global environment you need to be aware of:

- your personal style and how this may be viewed by people from other countries

- the way people from other cultures expect to be managed

- how your style will be perceived and the possibility that international colleagues or clients may feel confused and unsure about your actions.

BUSINESS IN SOCIETY

30% of the Australian population was born overseas.

43% of Australians have at least one parent who was born overseas.

Australians speak over 200 languages.

BUSINESS IN SOCIETY

Catering for diversity is about creating a workplace environment in which people can achieve their full potential. It is about creating an organisation where a broad range of abilities, talents and perspectives are valued and supported. It is part of the process of creating an organisation geared towards strong business performance.

From The Business Case for Diversity published by Diversity@work

Ways to use diversity in the workplace for business success

Ways in which diversity in the workplace can be used to create business success include:

- expanding and forming new markets

- advertising in community languages

- using bilingual staff for sales campaigns and to train other staff on cross-cultural communication

- including images of customers from a range of backgrounds in advertising material

- using cultural festivals as marketing opportunities

- marketing products popular in ethnic niche markets to mainstream Australia which has become increasingly open to new experiences and styles

- employing professional bilingual staff for international business trips

- using bilingual staff to provide client service in the first language of customers
- developing translated information for service information and instructions for use.

INNOVATION AND OPERATIONS

IBM prides itself on their diverse workforce. They have ongoing programs to educate staff about diversity and to identify the value a diverse workforce brings to the company. Cultural diversity education initiatives involve professional development and general staff awareness.

Professional development prepares managers for business with clients or colleagues from another country. If a manager needs to travel to a country, professional development offers information on customs and business meeting protocol.

Other workshops train employees in:

- why certain behaviours and communication styles fail in some cultures
- how to address cultural differences and prevent misunderstandings
- managing culturally diverse teams.

YouTube
A Peacock in the Land of Penguins CRM

Examples of how IBM's cultural diversity strategy raises employee awareness of different cultures include:

- celebrating Chinese New Year for Sydney employees
- diversity calendar showing dates of cultural significance that might be relevant to employees and business partners
- a program where employees exchange a public holiday for a significant cultural holiday.

Legal and ethical requirements

An employer has legal obligations to manage diversity in a positive way. The following legislation prohibit discrimination and encourage workplaces to be tolerant and to recognise the differences that exist in the workforce and give all people the opportunity to achieve to the best of their ability:

- *Australian Human Rights Commission Act*
- *Age Discrimination Act*
- *Sex Discrimination Act*
- *Racial Discrimination Act*
- *Racial Hatred Act*
- *Disability Discrimination Act*
- *Workplace Gender Equality Act 2012*
- *Fair Work Act* and National Employment Standards (NES)
- State-based anti-discrimination and OH&S laws

The ASX Corporate Governance Council has introduced a requirement for listed companies to adopt and disclose a diversity policy and measurable objectives relating to gender or explain why they have not done so. From 1 January 2011, Australian-listed companies will be encouraged to disclose in their annual reports:

- the company's performance in achieving gender objectives set out by the board

- the proportion of women on the board, in senior management and employed throughout the whole organisation.

The *Workplace Gender Equality Act 2012* requires private sector employers with 100 or more employees to submit a report to the Workplace Gender Equality Agency detailing the gender mix of staff at all levels of the organisation and the strategies in place to achieve gender equity in the workplace, including career opportunities and pay equity.

YouTube
Workplace Gender Equality Agency explaining the gender pay gap

---

INNOVATION AND OPERATIONS

The University of South Australia has an Equity and Diversity Unit, which plans activities including:

- promotion of the anti-racism policy and distribution of a booklet explaining the impact of the policy
- preparation and distribution of pamphlets for staff and students about the Equal Opportunity Act and its significance for people from other cultures
- posters and postcards with anti-racist, pro-diversity messages
- preparing seminars and gatherings at which staff and visitors address racism, at University, faculty and campus levels.

Managing diversity for business growth

To benefit from diversity, a culture in which all employees feel free to contribute ideas must be established. This will encourage all staff to share their ideas and opinions, give feedback and participate in decision making.

Strategies to do this include:

- Ensure everyone is heard – hold meetings, organise consultation, have formal and informal ways to collect feedback and suggestions.

- Make it safe to propose ideas – this will encourage creativity and looking at problems in innovative ways.

- Give employees authority to make decisions – if they have the responsibility for making decisions they will feel more valued by the business and be more committed to the outcome.

- Share credit for success – acknowledge the contribution of all staff.

- Give constructive feedback – work with staff on their ideas and give them support to develop them.

- Implement feedback from staff – participation and innovation will be encouraged if employees see that their input is valued and acted upon.

Managing diversity can create market opportunities. A diverse workforce reflects and better understands the diverse community and consumers in the marketplace. If there is at least one member of a team with traits (ethnicity, age, ability) in common with the target market, the entire team will understand the target market.

By bringing together individuals from different backgrounds and experiences in work teams, businesses can more effectively market to consumers from different racial and ethnic backgrounds, women, people with disabilities, and consumers who are gay or transgender. Diversifying the workforce helps businesses increase their market share.

An example is the situation where a customer with English as a second language makes a complaint or enquires about products and services with a staff member with the same language background. They can converse in the same language, reduce misunderstanding and more easily identify the needs of the customer. The customer feels more comfortable with the staff member and is more likely to return in the future.

This also applies on a global scale where managers may be in complex contract negotiations with potential partners in other countries. If they share the same language, negotiations are more effective. Staff knowledge of the culture of the target market will also help refine marketing strategies.

Having a diverse workforce and a workplace that is free from discrimination will decrease staff turnover and help build high employee satisfaction and loyalty. This will reduce the disruption and costs of staff turnover.

Bringing together workers with different qualifications, backgrounds and experiences will lead to effective problem solving on the job. People with similar backgrounds and experience will look at problems in similar ways. Diversity will bring together people who have worked in small and large workplaces, in similar companies in different countries and who may have faced the problem before.

Diversity in the workplace is necessary to be competitive in a globalised world. Capitalising on the unique talents and contributions that diverse workers bring to the workplace will make Australian companies more competitive in the global economy.

CHAPTER 13
Unit 3 People activities

'The greatest danger in times of turbulence is not
the turbulence – it is to act with yesterday's logic.'
– Peter Drucker –

Topic study

1. Successful change depends on what two aspects?
2. What are three examples of change in a workplace?
3. What are two examples of critical success factors that can increase the likelihood of successful change?
4. What three things should management consider to overcome resistance to change?
5. What are two causes of resistance to change?
6. What are two things management can do to prepare staff for change?
7. Describe the three stages of Lewin's change process.
8. What are three main factors that cause change to be unsuccessful?
9. What is Force Field Analysis?
10. List the eight steps of Kotter's change process.
11. What are three aspects of diversity?
12. What are two ways to use diversity in the workplace for business success?
13. What is an example of legislation that has an impact on the management of diversity?
14. What is an example of a strategy to build a culture that values diversity?
15. What is the *Workplace Gender Equality Act 2012*?

Business research

1. Preparing for change

Two change models are Lewin's three stages and Kotter's eight steps. In pairs discuss both models and use a table like the one below to compare the models. Classify the eight steps into one of the three stages that they relate to the best. In which stage would you implement the step?

Lewin's stages	Kotter's steps
Unfreeze	
Change	
Refreeze	

2. Preparing for change

Choose two reasons for resistance to change. Develop strategies that a company could use to overcome the resistance. Use the following action plan format to detail your strategies.

Reason for resistance	Strategies	Who is responsible?

3. Global change and adaptation

Apple launched its iPad 2 simultaneously in 25 countries, on the same day, with the same message and advertising; a consistent marketing proposition around the globe.

i.   What is positioning (in terms of marketing and business)? Describe it in terms of a global company.

ii. Discuss how marketing standardisation and adaptation can be used to establish a global position.

iii. How can a product's position become an asset in international marketing?

iv. How would you describe Apple's global position?

v.   What additional challenges does international positioning involve?

Response

1. Force Field Analysis

Conduct a force field analysis to analyse diversity in an Australian company that wants to grow globally. Evaluate the benefits and challenges of having a diverse workforce. Use the following action plan format to detail your strategies.

Reason for resistance	Strategies	Who is responsible?

2. Preparing for change and Innovation

You run a medical services business that operates in Australia and through outlets in Singapore and Jakarta. You have decided to innovate and replace handwritten patient records with an electronic system. Instead of handwritten patient forms and written doctor note, surgeries will use an intranet to record consultations, print prescriptions, update and access patient files. It is a big change from the manual, hand written documentation that has been used for years.

i. Describe the benefits this innovation can bring to the company.

ii. Discuss possible challenges the company may face when implementing this innovation. Why could there be resistance to change?

iii. Develop a change strategy to implement the innovation using Lewin's three stages of change – Unfreeze, Change, Refreeze.

3. Diversity

Investigate diversity in Australia and find recent statistics regarding the ethnic and religious composition of Australia's population. Present your findings as graphs.

i. Choose one ethnic and one religious group.

ii. Develop three strategies a company could use to leverage diversity for business growth (refer to the suggested 'Ways to use diversity in the workplace for business success' in **Chapter 12**).

iii. Describe the strategies and design materials that could be used, for example advertisements, posters.

The 4 Plan

Using a plan to organise your work will focus you on your main tasks and make your research more efficient.

- Introduction: identify the topic, theme or purpose of your presentation and list four key points or aspects of the topic.

- For each key point or aspect list the Boolean search terms you will use to find information.

- Record two or more sources for each point to show what you read to learn about them.

- Make recommendations based on what you have learned.

Introduction

Sources | **Sources** | **Sources** | **Sources**

Recommendations

CHAPTER 14
Unit Three
Examination questions

'We are moving toward a global economy. One way of approaching that is to pull the covers over your head. Another is to say: It may be more complicated but that's the world I am going to live in, I might as well be good at it.'

– Phil Condit –

The structure of the examination for Year 12 ATAR Business Management and Enterprise is:

Section	Number of questions	Number that must be answered	Marks per question	Suggested working time in minutes	Total marks
1: Short Answer	6	6	10	100	60
2: Extended Answer	3	2	20	80	40
				Total	100

This chapter contains short answer and extended answer questions that reflect the content in Unit 3 of the Year 12 ATAR course. Students can use these questions to prepare for the ATAR exam.

Questions from this chapter can also be used to construct an examination for school based assessment.

Short answer questions

Question 1

i.   What is globalisation? What are two opportunities globalisation may offer an Australian company? (3 marks)

ii. What are three ways technology can assist a company to expand globally? (3 marks)

iii. Explain how transfer pricing is used to minimise tax in a global market. (4 marks)

Question 2

i. What is ethics? Discuss why global business may create an ethical dilemma. (4 marks)

ii. How can offshore labour create ethical difficulties for an Australian company? (3 marks)

iii. Discuss two other examples of how operating globally can create an ethical problem. (3 marks)

Question 3

i. What is standardisation when entering a foreign market? (3 marks)

ii. Explain the alternative to standardisation for market entry. (3 marks)

iii. Discuss the difference between standardisation and adaptation using product and positioning. (4 marks)

Question 4

i. What is a 'strategic alliance'? (2 marks)

ii. Explain the difference between a merger and an acquisition. (4 marks)

iii. Explain the difference between joint venture and franchising. (4 marks)

Question 5

i. What are two risks a company faces when involved in international transactions? (4 marks)

ii. How can insurance be used to manage risk in international business? What is an example of a risk that can be insured against? (3 marks)

iii. What is hedging? What are two forms of hedging that could be used to manage foreign exchange risk? (3 marks)

Question 6

i. Discuss the difference between process innovation and product innovation. (4 marks)

ii. Discuss two benefits innovation can bring to an international business. (4 marks)

iii. How can intellectual property protection help a business exploit innovation? (2 marks)

Question 7

i. Discuss two reasons why there may be resistance to change in a workplace. (4 marks)

ii. Describe how Force Field Analysis is used. (4 marks)

iii. Why is it important to create a sense of urgency for successful change? (2 marks)

Question 8

iv. What is diversity in the workplace? List three examples of how a workplace can be diverse. (4 marks)

v. What are two laws that regulate the management of diversity. (2 marks)

vi. What are two ways a diverse workforce can help a business expand globally? (4 marks)

Extended answer questions

Question 1

Diversity management is key to growth in the competitive global marketplace. Companies cannot compete if they lack cultural intelligence. Companies must embrace diversity and build a workplace that reflects the diverse community in which they operate.

i. Discuss four differences an Australian company may find when they expand into foreign markets. (4 marks)

ii. Explain three ways a company can adapt their marketing strategies to compete more effectively in global markets. (6 marks)

iii. Describe four ways Australian managers can develop their cultural intelligence. (4 marks)

iv. Discuss two risks an Australian company faces when operating internationally and how these risks can be managed. (6 marks)

Question 2

> 'To build and sustain brands people love and trust, one must focus—not only on today but also on tomorrow. It's not easy…but balancing the short and long term is key to delivering sustainable, profitable growth—growth that is good for our shareholders but also good for our consumers, our employees, our business partners, the communities where we live and work, and the planet we inhabit.'
>
> Irene Rosenfeld, CEO Kraft

Analyse and discuss the above quotation in relation to:

i. Three benefits of globalisation. (6 marks)

ii. Three impacts of globalisation. (6 marks)

iii. Ethics and how ethics are different to laws and regulations in a global marketplace. (4 marks)

iv. Two ethical issues global businesses face. (4 marks)

Question 3

The Nobel Prize-winning economist Professor Joseph Stiglitz has warned Australia of hidden dangers in the proposed free trade agreement called the TPP, or Trans-Pacific Partnership:

'This trade agreement is not just lowering tariffs but setting the rules of the game for the 21st century. Rules about regulation, rules about drugs. These are really critical aspects for the running of our society, affecting our health, our environment.'

i. Outline what a free trade agreement is and what it aims to do. Give an example of a free trade agreement that includes Australia. (4 marks)

ii. Explain how tariffs have an impact on trade between countries. (2 marks)

iii. Discuss two ways an Australian business could benefit from a free trade agreement. (4 marks)

iv. Outline what the Investor State Dispute Settlement (ISDS) involves. Explain why there is concern about the ISDS. Give an example of an issue that involves ISDS. (6 marks)

v. Discuss whether Australia should enter into free trade agreements or use laws and regulations to protect Australian businesses from foreign competition. (4 marks)

Question 4

New technological developments are creating totally new industries. These breakthroughs have come from advances in nanotechnology, research and development, and mobile technology. Companies are tackling these changes by attempting to anticipate how they will affect consumer trends. The implication for innovation in technology is there will be fewer barriers for virtual businesses, more competition and the ability to use technology to create and enter new global markets.

i. What is innovation? Describe two types of innovation. (5 marks)

ii. Describe two benefits of innovation. (4 marks)

iii. Innovation involves change. Outline two tools a company could use to prepare their staff for change. (6 marks)

iv. Discuss three reasons for resistance to change. (5 marks)

UNIT FOUR
CHAPTER 15
Culture and ethics

'Its not hard to make decisions when you know what your vales are.'
– Roy Disney –

CULTURAL CONSIDERATIONS

We can understand culture in three ways as shown here.

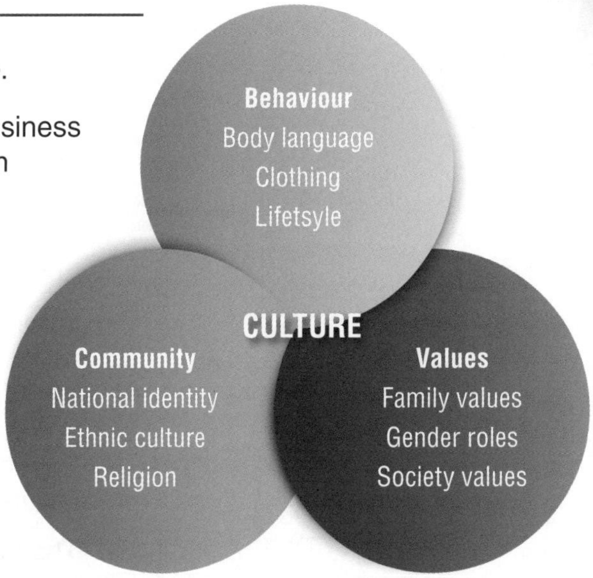

Understanding culture will help you to build long-term business relationships and more effective marketing strategies. An understanding of the management and communication styles used in different countries is important if you want to be successful at a global level. A lack of knowledge about international business practices is a cause of conflicts and misunderstanding between managers from different countries.

Cultural knowledge and understanding is applied on a personal level and when incorporated into business strategy and planning will increase the likelihood of business success.

This chapter looks at key aspects of culture that have an impact on global business.

Behaviour
Body language
Clothing
Lifetsyle

CULTURE

Community
National identity
Ethnic culture
Religion

Values
Family values
Gender roles
Society values

Customs and etiquette

Phone etiquette

- Don't interrupt a face-to-face conversation with someone by taking a call or texting.
- At a business lunch, a mobile device shouldn't be part of the place setting. Keep it stashed in a jacket pocket, handbag or briefcase.
- Have a professional ringtone to convey a professional image.
- Take personal calls at work in a private place and keep personal calls to a minimum.

Business etiquette

Some examples of business etiquette from around the world follow.

Brazil
- Brazilians stand very close and use physical contact during conversations.
- Closeness inspires trust, and trust inspires long-term relationships.

Canada
- Canadians tend to be extremely punctual and adhere to time schedules.

China
- Bring a small gift from your hometown or country to business meetings but do not use white, black or blue wrapping paper.
- Chinese people will decline a gift three times before finally accepting, so as not to appear greedy. You will have to continue to insist. You will be expected to go through the same routine if you are offered a gift.

India
- Indians are very polite. Avoid use of the word 'no' during business discussions; it's considered rude. Opt for terms such as 'we'll see', 'I will try' or 'possibly'.
- Don't order beef if attending a business meal in India. Cows are considered sacred in Indian culture.
- Traditional Indian food is eaten with the hands. When it is necessary to use your hands, use only your right hand, as the left hand is considered unclean.

Japan
- Expect to bow during an introduction and wait for them to initiate a handshake because it is less common.
- The exchange of business cards is a very formal act that kicks off meetings. Present your card with two hands while facing your colleague. Do not conduct a brief exchange or slide your card across the table.
- During meetings, the most senior person will lead discussions.
- When in a meeting the people of a similar level of authority and experience should sit opposite each other.

Different cultures have different levels of formality and place different emphasis on time constraints. In some parts of the world, more value is placed on a meeting resulting in positive outcomes than if it begins or ends on time. It is important that you accept that as long as you achieve your objectives, the way a meeting takes place is not so important.

Holidays and celebrations

If you are working overseas, make sure that you learn about local holidays and how they might have an impact on campaigns and other business projects. The month of Ramadan is important in many parts of the world, and, having critical deadlines during this month is challenging. If your target countries have a strong religious basis for their culture, make sure that you learn about the religion and its taboos, restrictions and ways that religious beliefs can work in your favour.

Communication protocols

Business people who know correct communication protocols show professionalism and can stand out from their competitors. If competing firms have similar products, prices and levels of service the customer may choose the business that seems to understand their culture the best.

YouTube
10 surprising ways to offend people in other countries

In some countries, like the United States and Germany, it is common for people to speak loudly and be more assertive or aggressive when sharing ideas or giving direction. In countries like Japan, people typically speak softly and are more passive about sharing ideas or making suggestions.

When interacting with people from different cultures, speaking in a neutral tone and making a conscious effort to be considerate of others' input, even if it is given in a manner to which you are not accustomed, can help build effective business communication.

Examples of communication protocols for **China**:

- Bowing or nodding is the common greeting; however, you may be offered a handshake. Wait for the Chinese to offer their hand first.
- Applause is common when greeting a crowd, the same is expected in return.
- Introductions are formal, and use formal titles.
- Often times Chinese will use a nickname to assist Westerners.
- Being on time is vital in China.
- Contacts should be made prior to your trip.
- Bring several copies of all written documents for your meetings.
- The decision-making process is slow. You should not expect to conclude your business swiftly.
- Many Chinese will want to consult with the stars or wait for a lucky day before they make a decision.
- Present and receive cards with both hands.
- Never write on a business card or put it in your wallet or pocket. Carry a small card case.
- The most important member of your company or group should lead important meetings, Chinese people value rank and status.
- Allow the Chinese people to leave a meeting first.

Examples of communication protocols for the **United States**:

- Offer a firm handshake, lasting 3-5 seconds, upon greeting and leaving.
- Maintain good eye contact during your handshake.
- If you are meeting several people at once, maintain eye contact with the person you are shaking hands with, until you are moving on the next person.
- Good eye contact during business and social conversations shows interest, sincerity and confidence.
- Good friends may briefly embrace, although the larger the city, usually the more formal the behavior.
- Introductions include one's title if appropriate, or Mr, Ms, Mrs and the full name.
- Business cards are generally exchanged during introductions, however, they may be exchanged when one party is leaving.

Examples of communication protocols for the **Australia**:

- Shake hands when meeting and when leaving.
- Exchanging business cards is common among professional workers.
- Australians are friendly and open, but directness and brevity are valued.
- Opinions are respected, and opinionated discussions are entertaining.
- Be an active listener, and ask if you do not understand something in the conversation.
- Do not hype yourself, your company or your information.
- Sightseeing and sports are good conversational topics.

Based on the culture in India following are some dos and don'ts for the workplace:

DO	DON'T
• Show respect for people including status, job titles and education.	• Discuss difficult political topics, eg. Pakistan or Kashmir.
• Be prepared to field personal questions including family.	• Refuse gestures of hospitality. These are opportunities to build business relationships, eg. invitations to meals, to visit local temples or other important cultural sites.
• Learn about general dietary rules for India's major religions, eg. beef and pork are off the menu for nearly all Indians.	• Assume that modern/Westernised Indian people have the same values as you. Beneath the surface, traditional cultural values may prevail.
• Learn about important Indian holidays, eg. Diwali and Holi.	
• Show knowledge and interest in Bollywood and cricket.	

Levels of education

The Organisation for Economic Co-operation and Development (OECD) studied the link between levels of education and economic growth. They studied 76 countries and prepared a list of global school rankings.

Singapore is on the top of the ranking, followed by Hong Kong with Ghana at the bottom. The UK is in 20th place, Australia is in 14th place and the US in 28th.

The top ten countries based on maths and science achievement at age 15:

1. Singapore
2. Hong Kong
3. South Korea
4. Japan
5. Taiwan
6. Finland
7. Estonia
8. Switzerland
9. Netherlands
10. Canada

Based on their research, the OECD estimated the growth in GDP of the lower ranked countries if all 15 year olds achieved a basic level of education, for example Ghana 3881% growth (or their GDP would expand by 38 times), South Africa 2624%, Peru 1076%, Colombia 910%.

They concluded that levels of education are a powerful predictor of the wealth that countries will produce over time. Poor education policies and practices result in countries being in what may be a permanent state of economic recession.

Global companies have taken advantage of poor education levels to sell their products. Tobacco companies target poor and developing countries (particularly children) because they do not have the same history of health education regarding the dangers of smoking as developed nations. While smoking is in decline in Australia and other developed nations, smoking is on the increase in developing nations. The Asia Pacific region is the world's biggest tobacco market with 30 million people expected to become smokers in recent years. The World Health Organisation calculates that of the 6 million people who will die from tobacco use this year, 80 per cent will be in the developing world.

Understanding the levels of education in a country will have an impact on business plans to expand globally. If there is a shortage of skilled labour in a country a company will need to base employees there or use financial packages to attract staff.

In developed countries there is a pool of skilled labour that can be accessed to fill positions and drive business growth. Poor and developing nations do not have the educational system in place to create that pool of skilled labour.

Differences in technology creates a digital divide. Differences in education creates a knowledge divide between countries.

One reason for the knowledge divide between nations is the level of investment in school education. There must be an early focus on basic literacy and primary education must be universally accessible. A good foundation or primary education leads to secondary and tertiary achievement.

Religious beliefs

Religious beliefs are part of the foundation of a country's culture. Religious values determine beliefs, the way people interact, lifestyles and in terms of marketing, sales and spending patterns.

Secular norms and practices have a religious basis, for example Christmas holidays and Easter. Countries have celebrations and holidays based on religious observances.

Religious beliefs may have minimal impact on business in some countries such as Australia, Europe and the US. In Muslim countries business is stopped five times a day for prayer. Business may also be affected during the month of Ramadam.

Following are examples of how religious beliefs can have an impact on business.

Muslim business ethics

In Islam, the basis of societal laws is the Qur'an. Islamic teachings strongly stress an ethical and moral code in human behaviour. Muslim ethics include avoidance of people's exploitation through lending them money at interest, and prohibitions against false advertising. Under Islamic laws, if a vendor sells an item by making false claims about it, the customer has the right to have the transaction cancelled.

Buddhist business ethics

The Buddhist business code and professional ethics are closely tied with respect for environment. Essentially, according to Buddhist teachings, ethical and moral principles are run by examining a certain action, which has to avoid any harm. Therefore some Buddhist texts emphasise on the role of enlightenment – one of the elements which prohibits occupations associated with violence (such as arms dealing).

Christian business ethics

In Christianity, the basis of this theology is the Old Testament and the New Testament. The Christian in commerce should not desire 'to get another's goods or labour for less than it is worth'. One must not try to obtain a good price for his own wares by extortion. If one is buying from the poor, 'charity must be exercised as well as justice'; purchaser must pay the full price that the goods are worth to him. Moreover, the purchaser shouldn't allow suffering of the vendor because he cannot stand firm for his price, but the vendor should offer a loan or persuade some one else to do so.

Jewish business ethics

Judaism, which relies on the Torah for its written law, has had a great impact on marketing and business ideology. Jewish culture, values and ideas have penetrated into many aspects of modern life including modern markets. Some points include: honesty in the market, fair pricing and business relations.

Indigenous business ethics

Indigenous enterprises often have to operate within an environment of complex social and cultural obligations. Indigenous business people have a desire to positively reflect Indigenous values in the surrounding mainstream community. Many Indigenous groups, particularly in remote areas, still maintain cultural practices. Cultural practice can sometimes be the product, for example tourism.

Global ethics

When operating in different nations, companies will encounter different values, beliefs and ethical standards. A company may work to spread their corporate culture and ethics to wherever they operate or adapt to the local standards for decision making.

This creates an ethical dilemma. Is it ethical to take advantage of the poor working conditions in a country to increase profit? To accept poor standards in a foreign country while complying to higher standards at home?

Companies have been criticised for basing their successful business model on cheap labour offshore. The prices we pay in developed countries are kept low because of global inequality.

Ethical issues in global business include:

- **Bribery:** involves payments offered to government officials and others to gain an advantage.

- **Lubrication:** involves a relatively small sum of cash, a gift or a service made to an official in a country to gain advantage or benefit, or to speed up a decision.

Bribery and corruption may seem like a straightforward legal issue. But, far from being illegal in some countries, it is part of the business culture. Management may be tempted to help the process along by making payments or gifts; it is important to be aware of the consequences. Unethical decisions may help in the short term but they can damage the company's reputation later and may lead to charges and legal action.

Corporate social responsibility – CSR

CSR is a strategic commitment by companies to ethical conduct and to consider the quality of life of employees, the local community and society when making business decisions.

When planning and operating a business, social and environmental concerns are considered as well as financial ones. A company looks beyond the demands of shareholders and is motivated by the needs of a broader range of stakeholders such as employees, customers, suppliers, the environment and people in the local community.

CSR involves:

- creating a safe and healthy workplace
- encouraging staff to find a good work/life balance
- corporate sponsorships and donations
- maintaining high standards of ethical business practice
- reducing waste and managing sustainable energy and resource consumption
- controlling its carbon footprint
- taking responsibility for the social impact of business operations.

Some of the benefits of CSR include:

- improved financial performance
- reduction in the exposure to risks in the business environment
- improved public image
- increased sales and customer loyalty
- better staff retention
- improved relations with governments
- reduced costs through waste reduction and process efficiency.

CSR is also known as the 'triple bottom line'. Companies evaluate their performance not just in terms of profit but also in terms of social and environmental outcomes.

Consumers and investors are interested in supporting responsible business practices and are demanding more information as to how companies address social and environmental issues.

There are businesses that provide investment advice based on ethical standards of companies. Investment companies also offer products such as managed funds and superannuation that focus on companies that have a strong commitment to environmental and social issues and do not derive income from products such as guns, tobacco or child labour.

Companies expanding their operations into other countries face scrutiny by local competitors and customers. If they are known for and can demonstrate social responsibility, a commitment to improving the community and society around them, it is more likely they will be accepted by the new market.

YouTube
CSR: Apple vs Microsoft

A company shows it is committed to CSR by not just complying with laws and regulations but by going beyond the minimum legal requirements. If a company has a good reputation and history of CSR, they may be given preferential treatment when applying for tenders or permits. If the company breaches laws and regulations the penalty may be minimised because of their good track record.

The reputation of a company will be based on how they treat the most vulnerable. The more a company is committed to CSR, the less they are exposing themselves to business risk. This could be risk to their public image because of bad press (for example Nike and sweatshops, Nestle and marketing baby formula in poor countries), financial risk or environmental risk.

Our demand for cheaper products, more value and choice means that companies will always be looking for cheaper suppliers and materials. This may lead them to consider unethical sources such as illegally harvested timber, food manufactured under questionable quality and health standards, or exploited labour. This is where CSR plays a role. By looking beyond short-term profit a company will resist unethical options because they are motivated by long-term success and what is best for society.

> **BUSINESS IN SOCIETY**
> Kimberly-Clark Australia markets leading household brands such as Kleenex and Huggies. They installed a power cogeneration facility at their factory in South Australia. The waste heat in the exhaust of the gas turbine is captured and used to replace natural gas to drive their production process. The aim is to reduce carbon dioxide emissions by up to 80,000 tonnes and achieve savings of $8.8 million.

International labour standards

Globalisation has provided opportunities for many countries but it has also led to increased inequality and a growing gap between the world's richest and poorest nations. While companies use low-cost countries to grow their profit there is still poverty, social instability and conflict. The low-cost countries do not necessarily see the benefits of globalisation. Which is the point. If poor countries have better employment standards, and comparable pay and conditions and safety, then they would no longer be attractive as targets for offshoring and outsourcing.

To ensure fair treatment and increased prosperity for everybody around the world, basic global standards for labour are needed.

Since 1919, the International Labour Organisation (ILO) has been setting standards for employment to ensure that along with economic growth there is social justice, prosperity and peace for all. These international labour standards are legal instruments which define basic minimum standards in the world of work.

International labour standards are either conventions or recommendations.

- **Conventions:** legally binding international treaties, ratified by the ILO's member nations.

- **Recommendations:** non-binding guidelines which provide detailed suggestions on how conventions could be applied.

The ILO has 188 conventions and 199 recommendations. There are four aspects of labour standards that are considered to be fundamental to social justice and prosperity:

- The elimination of discrimination related to employment and occupation
- The effective abolition of child labour
- The elimination of all forms of forced or compulsory labour
- Freedom of association and the effective recognition of the right to collective bargaining

The ILO estimates there are 317.4 million children aged 5 to 17 engaged in work, including 190.7 million in the age group from 5 to 14 years. 'Child labour' is a well- defined concept. It excludes children 12 years and older who are doing light work for a few hours a week and children 15 years and above whose work is not classified as hazardous. The ILO understands that because of poverty, social conditions and the absence of government support (such as unemployment benefits, financial support for children and families) children may have to work. But they have strict standards to try and prevent the exploitation of children.

ILO estimate that child labour declined by 30% between 2000 and 2012. Still, 11% of the world's children are in situations that deprive them of their right to go to school without interference from work.

Most child workers are employed in the clothing industry making the clothes that are sold in developed countries.

BUSINESS IN SOCIETY

Fast fashion is exemplified by brands such as Cotton On, Zara, H&M and Forever 21. Fast fashion refers to clothing manufactured cheaply in poor countries so consumers in wealthy countries can always have lots of choice. In order to maintain the supply of clothing at a profitable level, cheap labour and child labour is used.

Child labour is prohibited as defined in the ILO Minimum Age Convention and the ILO Worst Forms of Child Labour Convention. Child labour is a violation of fundamental human rights. It has been shown to perpetuate poverty across generations as children grow up without access to education or decent health care.

The Minimum Age Convention sets the following minimum standards for work:

The minimum age at which children can start work

Hazardous work Any work which is likely to jeopardise children's health, safety or morals should not be done by anyone under the age of 18	18 (16 under strict conditions)
Basic minimum age The minimum age for work should not be below the age for finishing compulsory schooling, which is generally 15	15
Light work Children between the ages of 13 and 15 years old may do light work, as long as it does not threaten their health and safety, or hinder their education or vocational orientation and training.	13 to 15

The Worst Forms of Child Labour Convention requires member nations to eliminate all forms of slavery or practices similar to slavery. For example:

- the sale and trafficking of children
- debt bondage (a child is forced to work until the debts of their family are repaid)

- forced or compulsory labour
- recruitment of children for use in armed conflict
- the use, procuring or offering of children for prostitution and pornography
- the use, procuring or offering or children for illicit activities such as the production and trafficking of drugs
- work which is likely to harm the health, safety or morals of children.

Australia is a founding member of the ILO and a major contributor to the work of the organisation through the Australian Government-ILO Partnership Agreement (2010-2015). Australia contributes to projects in Indonesia, Papua New Guinea, Timor and Pacific Island countries. Australia has ratified 63 ILO conventions.

The ILO has formal complaints procedures under Articles 24 and 26 of the ILO Constitution. It includes the establishment of a Commission of Inquiry in the most serious cases of alleged non-compliance, and referral to the International Court of Justice.

YouTube
The true cost of cheap clothing

> **BUSINESS IN SOCIETY**
> The Australian Ethical Fashion Guide ranks 41 brands available in Australia on how well they prevent worker exploitation and modern slavery. It looks at three key issues:
> - an overall grade on labour management practices
> - whether companies pay a living wage
> - whether companies do enough to avoid using Uzbekistani cotton which is picked using forced child labour.

Environmental sustainability

Companies today are making an effort to put sustainable practices into action. They are motivated by protecting the environment and society and by creating goodwill for their brands.

Globalisation has increased the level at which businesses rely on each other to deliver products and services to the market. Improved technology, communications and distribution channels have increased the reach of Australian businesses. Business decisions and activities can have an impact on other countries not just locally.

Green initiatives can also save money by such things as reducing packaging materials, minimising transportation costs and energy-efficient lighting.

Companies can manage sustainability proactively in their supply chain; for example, by ensuring they do not import and retail timber that has been illegally harvested. Companies can make a commitment to sustainability by demanding sustainability from their suppliers.

> **BUSINESS IN SOCIETY**
> Kimberly-Clark Australia markets leading household brands such as Kleenex and Huggies. They installed a power cogeneration facility at their factory in South Australia. The waste heat in the exhaust of the gas turbine is captured and used to replace natural gas to drive their production process. The aim is to reduce carbon dioxide emissions by up to 80,000 tonnes and achieve savings of $8.8 million.

CHAPTER 16
The global economy

'The word "overseas" has no place in Honda's vocabulary,
because it sees itself as equidistant from all its key customers.'
– Kenichi Ohma –

When planning and operating a business you must assess the external macro environment for threats and opportunities. There are economic factors that impact on business operations on a domestic scale. It gets more complex when you consider economic factors in different countries when planning global business growth.

The economic factors explored in this chapter are:

- economic activity
- interest rates
- discretionary spending
- currency fluctuations.

Economic activity

In general economic activity involves the production, distribution, buying and selling of products and services. One way it is measured is by a country's gross domestic product (GDP). The strength of economic activity and estimated future levels can significantly affect business growth and profits, inflation and interest rates.

An economic expansion is an increase in the level of economic activity, and of the goods and services available. It is a period of economic growth as measured by a rise in real GDP. The explanation of fluctuations in aggregate economic activity between economic expansions and contractions is one of the primary concerns of macroeconomics.

Economic expansion is an upturn in economic activity. Economic activity is influenced by factors such as:

GLOBAL	DOMESTIC
• global prosperity	• government policies
• weather conditions	• interest rates
• technological change	• availability of credit
• conflict	• laws and regulations
	• government incentives

Economic contraction and expansion relate to the overall output of all goods and services, while the terms inflation and deflation refer to increasing and decreasing prices of commodities, goods and services in relation to the value of money.

Consumer confidence is also influenced by economic activity. If the economy is strong, spending is high, unemployment is low then consumers and businesses are confident that their level of income will continue and grow into the future. They are more likely to borrow and spend. This keeps economic activity going and growing.

If economic activity is low or slowing, entering the market has increased risk. Success is more likely in countries where economic activity is strong and expected to continue to grow.

Australian companies have prospered from the strong growth in China's economic activity. Chinese companies are employing more people and living standards are improving. There has been a huge demand for Australian raw materials to build housing, factories and infrastructure such as roads. It seems now that the economic activity in China has plateaued and perhaps is slowing. This means that the sales and income earned by Australian businesses will fall.

It is a delicate balance. If economic activity is strong and spending keeps increasing, inflation may become an issue. Interest rates are used as a tool or lever to try and balance economic growth and inflation.

 YouTube
The circular flow

BUSINESS IN SOCIETY

The Kimberley region in WA has a diverse economy:; mining, construction, tourism, retail, fishing, agriculture and pearling. Economic activity in agriculture was valued at $230 million in 2011-12. Mining production was valued at $1.1 billion in 2012-2013. The Kimberley pearl industry was valued at $67.5 million in 2008-09. In tourism over the last few years there has been an average of 292,600 domestic and international visitors to the Kimberley annually. The total value of tourism economic activity was $327 million.

Interest rates

The interest rate level is an indicator of the strength of an economy. It is the cost of borrowing money. Consumers and businesses borrow money to purchase products and services and to make investments.

Domestically, interest rates have an impact on how easy it is to fund business expansion, including expansion into overseas markets. If interest rates are high, debt repayments will be high. This will have an impact on cash flow and the ability of a business to borrow money to finance business growth. High interest rates will also limit the borrowing of consumers and businesses and their spending on products and services. This fall in demand and sales will impact on the income and profit of businesses.

The interest rate is set by a central agency in an economy. The banks and other financial institutions add their profit margin and offer that rate to consumers and businesses to borrow money.

If economic activity is slowing or the economy is shrinking, central agencies will decrease interest rates to try and stimulate activity. By making loans more affordable the hope is that consumers and businesses will borrow more, spend more and economic activity will increase.

Inflation

Inflation is bad for economic activity. Inflation is a measure of the increase in price of a bundle of typical consumer goods – the shopping basket. People and businesses are earning the same amount of money but they can buy less because of increasing prices – their purchasing power decreases.

Inflation can happen because of easy access to debt, leading to demand for products and services exceeding the supply or because there is a rapid increase in the costs of materials and supplies. Businesses have to spend more manufacturing and selling their products and services and the cost increase is added to their prices to maintain profitability.

In good economic times prices also rise. When people have secure employment and high wages, they will be more confident about their future income, more likely to spend than save money and are also more likely to borrow money. They are more willing to spend. Businesses respond by increasing their prices because they know customers have the ability to keep purchasing despite the price increases.

The higher the inflation rate, the more interest rates are likely to rise. Central agencies such as the Reserve Bank of Australia and the US Federal Reserve increase interest rates to reduce the amount of discretionary spending. If consumers and businesses have to use more money to repay debt they will have less to spend on products and services.

Spending will also be limited because of the high cost of borrowing money. Demand will fall, supply will exceed demand and prices should decrease.

The impact of interest rates on spending and investment occurs in all countries. If interest rates are high in the target country then the consumers and businesses there will limit their spending. Economic activity will be slower and the success of new businesses and launches of new products and services will be less likely to succeed. Low interest rates stimulate spending and may mean that business success is more likely.

Discretionary spending

As the economies of countries develop there are more people earning decent wages in stable employment. This means that they have greater discretionary income. This is the amount they have left over once they pay life's essentials such as food, rent, clothing, education and taxes (non-discretionary spending). The more discretionary income someone has the more they can spend on goods and services and stimulate economic growth.

Part of assessing market potential is to measure and estimate discretionary income in the population and in target markets.

China will record the highest real growth in consumer expenditure, at 67.6% over the 2013-2020 period, reflecting the country's shift from an export-dependent economy to a consumption-driven one. Nevertheless, despite rising disposable incomes and spending, China will still have the lowest proportion of discretionary spending in total consumer expenditure – at 59.3% in 2020, compared to 57.1% in 2013. This partly reflects the strong inclination by Chinese consumers to delay immediate consumption in favour of saving for the future, due to the inadequate provision of social welfare and also the high costs of living in China, especially in major cities.

By contrast, Brazilian consumers place a great importance on living in the moment, as demonstrated by the consistently high proportion of discretionary spending in total consumer expenditure in Brazil. Despite slowing economic growth since the 2008-2009 global financial crisis, consumer expenditure in Brazil has continued to grow robustly, driven by a consumer credit boom.

Consumers continue 'tightening their belts', according to the Boston Consulting Group's 2013 Global Consumer Sentiment Survey of more than 35,000 people in 20 countries. Nearly half of the consumers surveyed in developed economies do not expect economic improvement in the next several years, and 46 per cent said they plan to cut discretionary spending. Translation: businesses shouldn't expect a return to the free-spending days before the recession. Global consumers are concerned about job security, personal finances and the health of the economy.

Currency fluctuations

From political turmoil to a natural disaster, there are plenty of factors that cause a currency's value to rise and fall. When a business engages in international business transactions — such as importing, exporting and paying foreign employees — swings in currency value can have a significant impact on the bottom line.

Market fluctuations can affect everything from purchasing power to operating costs, making it difficult for businesses to predict profits and losses. If exchange rates take an unfavorable turn, an international business may end up paying more or receiving less from its partners and overseas customers.

If you are a business owner with products or services offered overseas, you should be very aware of the foreign exchange rates comparing Shekels to other currencies. While many companies do have finance or accounting employees or advisors who may follow these rates, many businesses, and small business owners in particular, are not giving enough heed to the rates and the effects they can have on the business.

The rates are moving every few seconds, and in just a few minutes the rate can move in either direction very quickly and without warning. That leaves any business susceptible to potential losses on a number of fronts.

Therefore, organisations have to evaluate the risks of doing business on an international level. For example, McDonald's increased sales and profit in Europe but, because of a strong US dollar, the contribution was lower when the Euros were converted into USD.

If the Australian dollar <u>rises</u> against foreign currency	If the Australian dollar <u>falls</u> against foreign currency
• Goods exported from Australia will become more expensive • Tourists will find Australia more expensive • Consumers are more likely to buy cheaper imports than Australian made goods	• Goods imported into Australia will become more expensive in AUD • People travelling to Australia will be able to spend more • Australian made goods will be more affordable than imported goods

Here is an example. A customer wants to buy a computer online from a business in Singapore. It costs SGD1000. Although that is a set price in Singapore, how much it costs in Australian dollars depends upon the exchange rate at the time of the sale.

Singapore price	AUD exchange rate	AUD dollars
$1000	75c	$1333
$1000	$1.02	$980

When the exchange rate is high the customers spends $980. If the exchange rate is lower the customer must spend more AUD to pay the same price in SGD.

YouTube
The global economy

CHAPTER 17
Business funding

'It's not how much you earn, it's how much you owe.'
– Ted Turner –

FINANCIAL INTERMEDIARIES

There are two main aspects of a financial system: money deposited into saving and investment accounts and money that is distributed through loans and credit. Financial intermediaries bring the two together, accepting deposits and using that money to fund loans.

Examples of financial intermediaries are trading banks, credit unions, finance companies and merchant banks.

Trading banks

They offer a range of deposit, investment and loan accounts to individuals and businesses. The money collected from depositors and earned through investments is used to fund loans to customers.

Credit unions

Credit unions do not offer the full range of services and products of a bank. They may focus on one aspect of banking such as home or business lending or personal banking.

Finance companies

A finance company provides loans for businesses and consumers. But unlike a bank, a finance company does not accept deposits. A finance company organises funding from banks and other financial institutions at a certain interest rate and uses these funds to extend credit to customers. They earn profit by charging their customers a higher interest rate than what they are paying and charge customers loan fees and administration charges.

Merchant banks

Merchant banks focus on bringing together parties that have large amounts of capital to invest and parties that need large amounts of capital for acquisitions and projects. Merchant banks also invest their own funds in acquisitions and projects. Investment banks are similar to merchant banks but do not invest their own funds. They bring together the lenders and borrowers and facilitate the transaction for a fee.

SOURCES OF FUNDING

Internal funding

Retained profits

A business can use retained profits as an internal source of funding. A cash reserve is built up by allocating profit to be 'saved' and kept by the company. These funds can then be used to finance operations, pay off business debt or asset purchases. Retained profits allow a business to avoid increasing debt and the dilution of ownership that results from a share issue.

This option allows a company to maintain full control of the business rather than complicating management with creditors, new partners or outside investors. Involving financiers, investors or new owners in the company gives them a degree of influence in how the business is run.

It may be a slow process to accumulate the funds required. There may be a difference between profit on paper and cash flow due to sales and purchases being on credit. The business also needs cash to fund ongoing operations. If a company 'saves' too much profit there may not be enough capital to finance operations. A company may need to borrow funds anyway for working capital.

Sources of external funding

Debentures

Debentures are sold by a company in a similar way to shares. A company will issue a prospectus detailing their financial performance, future plan and the details of the debentures. People or other companies apply for the debentures and at a later date they are issued to the successful applicants. Debentures pay a fixed amount of interest at regular intervals over a fixed period of time. Like shares, debentures can be sold on the open market. They have value because of their guaranteed income they earn.

Unlike shares, debenture holders are not owners of the company and do not have voting rights. A company can raise money without giving up ownership, with fixed costs that can be planned for over the long term.

Share capital

A privately owned business can raise money by becoming a company. To form a privately owned company, shares are sold to a limited number of owners or parties who want to make an investment and be involved in running the business. A publicly listed company raises money for operations and growth by selling shares to the public.

Shareholders put funds into a company by paying for a new issue of shares and/or through retained profits. Shareholders are entitled to a share of company profits through the payment of dividends. Dividends are not mandatory, they are paid if the Board of Directors believes the company can afford it. By not paying dividends profits can be retained in the company.

Trade credit

Suppliers may offer their customers a period of time to pay their invoices, perhaps 30 or 60 days. This gives a business an interest free period to delay payment and get the money together to pay the bill. A longer period may be negotiated, or instalment payment terms. In effect, the supplier is financing your business – you get the goods and services without payment up front.

Venture capital

Wealthy individuals and companies offer long-term loans for businesses. A bank may not agree to lend capital to a new business or for a new product or service if it seems too risky. The entrepreneur starting the business may approach venture capitalists for funding. Venture capitalists may be more willing to take the risk for long-term gain. Because a significant amount of money is at stake, the venture capitalists will make a loan on the condition that they become part owners and be involved in the management of the business.

Because a new venture is being financed, there is a high risk of losing the entire investment and it might take a long time before any profits and returns are earned. But there is also the prospect of high profits and a substantial return on the investment if it succeeds. A venture capitalist will require a high expected rate of return on investments, to compensate for the high risk.

The role of venture capitalists is to:

- finance new and expanding businesses
- finance the development of new products and services
- bring management expertise to a business
- take on high risks with the expectation of high returns.

Examples of venture capitalists in Australia include:

- Macquarie Group
- Momentum Investment Group
- CVC Group.

There are also organisations that facilitate business relationships between people seeking venture capital and those seeking to invest their money, for example, the Australia Private Equity and Venture Capital Association.

> ### Momentum Investment Group[1]
>
> Momentum Investment Group has the following criteria for investment when considering applications for venture capital:
>
> $ **Management:** relevant commercial experience, ideally with previous success in building start-up ventures as well as detailed knowledge of target markets, customers and distribution channels.
>
> $ **Market Potential:** large, dynamic and readily accessible target markets. Market should preferably be global.
>
> $ **Common Interests:** entrepreneurs who aspire to become wealthy on the basis of their equity stake in the company, in tandem with all other shareholders.
>
> $ **Intellectual Property:** the technologies are innovative, superior, protectable, and focused on meeting real market needs. The IP should preferably be owned by the company.
>
> $ **Exit Mechanism:** credible mechanisms for selling out Momentum's equity share; generally investments would be held for 3-5 years.
>
> $ **Hurdle Rate:** momentum seeks opportunities that can offer a minimum annual return of 58% compound.

Secured loans

A business can arrange a loan that is secured against assets it owns such as property, account receivable, vehicles or equipment. The amount a business can borrow, the interest rate charged and the term of the loan depend partly on the security provided to the lender. A lender is more likely to approve a loan if there is security. If a business cannot repay the loan the lender can take control of the asset and sell it to try and recoup the debt.

Before a financial institution decides whether to extend a loan to a customer they consider the following factors:

- The purpose of the loan – is it likely to result in earnings that can finance debt repayments?

- The amount of the loan - the customer must state exactly how much he wants to borrow and be able to verify how they calculated the estimate (quotes, business and asset valuations)

- Other assets and income – can the customer draw on other income and assets to meet debt repayments?

- The duration of the loan – this will determine the type of loan, for example overdraft, lease for short term or a long-term mortgage.

Financial institutions

There is a range of financial institutions a business can go to for funding. Building societies and credit unions focus on personal lending and residential home loans. Institutions with a primary focus on business funding listed to follow.

---

1   http://www.momentumvc.com.au/docs/1300_f.htm

Type of financial institution	How it works
Bank	Works with a wide range of borrowers and lenders and provides a range of services including deposits, secured loans, managed funds and insurance, for example ANZ, Westpac, Bankwest.
Merchant bank	Provides loans to large companies. Provides advice and services regarding company finance, capital markets, foreign exchange and investment management, for example RMB Australia, Viaticus Capital.
Finance companies	Provides loans to small to medium businesses. They target high risk borrowers that may have been denied loans from banks. Finance companies protect themselves from risk by charging high interest and high fees with strict repayment terms, for example GE Capital, Finlease.

Governments

Governments aim to build the economy and encourage business and investment. One way in which governments encourage business growth is by providing grants and subsidies. A business may be eligible for a grant to finance activities such as business expansion, commercialisation of an innovation, research and development or exporting. The Federal Government has a grants and assistance finder to help businesses access government support.

INNOVATION AND OPERATIONS
The Federal Government is offering funding for businesses to help them pay for training that will help them and their staff to:
- enter new markets
- adopt emerging technologies
- enter export markets

Crowd funding

An emerging source of external funding is crowd funding. A business idea is promoted and calls for investment are made. Anyone can invest and there may be a range of benefits depending on the amount invested. Benefits may be a return on investment, exclusive rights to the product or service or involvement in the business. Feature films have been financed through crowd funding and investors get to work in the film as an extra. The business start-up would have a financial target that is reached by receiving small contributions from many people.

Examples of crowd funding include Venture Crowd and Kickstarter.

BUSINESS IN SOCIETY
Since Kickstarter was launched in 2009: 5.3 million people have pledged $908million, funding 53,000 creative projects.

YouTube
Consumer banks vs. Investment banks vs. Merchant banks

CHAPTER 18
Factors that affect global success

'Globalisation is like creating a round-toed shoe that fits people
with all types of feet. It is not as comfortable as a perfectly fitted shoe
and doesn't fit snugly, but can be worn by many people.'
– David DeBry –

IMPACTS ON GLOBAL SUCCESS

When planning a global venture you must consider many factors. It is far more complex than a domestic business. Domestically you must consider markets, competition, laws and regulations in different states or regions. But within a country, Australia is a good example, states are adopting national legal and regulatory frameworks to standardise how businesses must operate.

The factors that affect global business are more complex because they involve the culture, technology, politics, laws and regulations of different countries with diverse histories, institutions and governments. Understanding these factors is vital for identifying opportunities for business growth and threats that can create barriers to success.

Political factors

When planning business growth, companies should consider the political environment in the target country. Political factors that can affect global business strategy include:

- the stability of the government
- the relationship of the foreign government with the Australian government
- governments passing legislation that can have an impact on business, for example tobacco plain packaging
- the government passing laws to protect consumers and the public interest
- government policies which influence economic development
- the government being a major consumer of goods and services
- government policies regarding privatisation which can create business opportunities.

Lack of political stability in a country affects business operations. Unstable countries may have riots, protests, looting and general disorder. These disrupt business operations. This conflict is often a product of poverty, corruption, civil unrest and warfare which create an environment that will not support business.

BUSINESS IN SOCIETY

In recent years Egypt has had political turmoil. Egypt's annual GDP growth slowed to 2.1% in 2013 from 5.1% in 2010. Indonesia encouraged business investment through improved political stability and business environment reforms. Foreign investment in Indonesia grew by 66.5% between 2008 and 2013.

When planning to expand globally a company can assess the political stability and risk of a country by asking the following questions:

- How stable is the government?
- Is it a democracy or a dictatorship?
- How drastically will the rules for business change if a new party comes into power?
- Is there a constitution and clear structure for government?
- How involved is the government in the private sector?
- Is there a well-established legal environment both to enforce policies and rules as well as to challenge them?
- How transparent is the government's decision-making process?

Political risks

Examples of political risks that must be considered when assessing global business growth include the following.

Ownership risk

When operations are threatened by government takeover or expropriation, owners may lose their offshore property. This is referred to as the nationalisation of business.

Operations risk

Government policies of the target country may create red tape and legal barriers to business operations such as finance, safety, employment, marketing and competition. These policies are known as operations risk.

Economic risk

Government policy may adversely affect currency exchange rates. Policies may result in currency devaluation or an economic downturn; for example, increasing interest rates, cutting government spending or restricting foreign capital and investment.

The purpose of free trade agreements is to remove or minimise these risks.

A government may want to encourage investment from foreign sources. Australia has policies, incentives and agreements to encourage new business. Foreign investment is regulated, but companies from overseas are encouraged to enter Australian markets. Australian governments also encourage domestic companies to enter global markets through providing information, establishing networks and funding.

Relationships between governments

The diplomatic and economic relationships between governments can have an impact on the success of global business. If there is an issue or disagreement between governments, one or both governments may retaliate or punish the other with economic restrictions. For example, Australia temporarily suspended live animal trade with Indonesia after evidence of animal cruelty was uncovered.

Free trade agreements and regional partnerships which make trade easier between countries are more likely to be developed and agreed to between countries with good relationships.

Countries that have similar cultures and shared histories often develop into trading partners which encourage cross-national business; European countries for example, and Australia with the US and New Zealand.

One way to look at giving foreign aid to developing countries now is that it creates trade partners in the future when their economy and standard of living improves. For this to occur the foreign aid must help develop the health, education and transport systems in a country so it has a foundation for economic growth. Foreign aid is often only enough to assist the governments of developing countries to manage crises and to maintain services not to develop economic capabilities.

Bailouts

Governments sometimes intervene in markets to 'save' failing businesses from closing. The aim is to give financial support to a business to prop it up so it can keep operating. This way governments can help a sector of its economy and hopefully minimise unemployment. During the global financial crisis governments bailed out large businesses such as banks and manufacturing companies. Governments bail out domestic businesses, so Australian businesses operating in foreign countries will not get the same financial support.

Bailouts have an impact on the market by allowing poorly-run companies to survive. Under normal market conditions these companies would go out of business.

Fiscal policy

Governments use policies to manage the collection and spending of money from taxes and other sources of revenue. The aim is to build a strong economy and a good standard of life for the majority of citizens. Fiscal policy deals with taxation and spending decisions that are used to help the economy. A government's taxation policy can have an impact on business profitability and create a business environment to encourage investment and growth. A high taxation environment, in countries

BUSINESS IN SOCIETY

Dubai does not tax the income of individuals or the profits of companies. Foreign companies operating in Dubai may be liable for tax under the taxation laws of their home countries.

such as Belgium and Finland, has an impact on the cash reserves companies have to invest and grow their business. Low-tax countries, such as Australia and Switzerland, will attract foreign companies and support business growth.

Legal factors

There can be major differences between the laws in different countries. Managers of a business must understand what the differences are and how they will affect the export and sale of products or services.

For example:

- the differences between legal systems
- differences in contract law
- patent registration and other intellectual property protections
- product liability laws and warranties
- product safety and labelling laws
- taxation, customs and quarantine laws
- consumer protection laws
- competition and foreign investment laws.

Patent registrations

To grow and succeed in business you must maintain a competitive advantage; to have something your competitors do not. One strategy to achieve this is to protect intellectual property (IP). If IP is protected no competitors can take sales and market share from you, they cannot compete directly with your products or services.

An important tool for IP protection are patents.

A patent is legally enforceable and gives the owner exclusive rights to manufacture and sell any device, substance, method or process that is new, inventive and useful.

To protect IP globally there are two options:

- Apply for a patent in countries individually – good if you only have a few target countries.

- Register a patent in multiple countries under the Patent Cooperation Treaty (PCT).

The PCT is administered by the World Intellectual Property Organization (WIPO) and takes effect in 148 countries. There are also regional patent agreements such as the European Patent Convention.

A patent is maintained as long as annual fees are paid. Patents must be updated if there are any changes to the device, substance, method or process.

You may find your patent is being breached and a company is making a copy of your patented product or service without permission or license. The first step is to send them a letter of warning to tell them to cease using your IP. This legal action can be followed by negotiations to settle damages out of court and court action to stop the offending company from making and selling products and services based on your IP, and to claim damages for lost sales and profits.

An Australia patent does not give you legal rights in other countries. If a company wants to protect their IP overseas they must register it in the target countries or under the PCT.

> **INNOVATION AND OPERATIONS**
> In 2012 there were over 30,000 patent applications in Australia; most made by applicants from the US, Japan and Germany.

International trademarks

If a trade mark is registered in Australia it is not protected overseas. Protecting trademarks globally can be done in two ways:

- The trademark is registered in countries individually
- A single registration is made under the Madrid Protocol

The Madrid Protocol

The Madrid Protocol is a treaty that provides international registration of a trademark. It is administered by the International Bureau (IB) of the World Intellectual Property Organisation (WIPO) in Geneva.

It is simply a method of facilitating the filing of trade mark applications in a number of countries simultaneously. All requests for protection in a Madrid Protocol contracting countries are examined according to the trademark legislation and laws existing in each designated country.

WIPO provides dispute resolution services as an alternative to court action:

- **Mediation:** an impartial mediator helps the parties in a dispute reach an agreement.
- **Arbitration:** parties agree to work with an arbitrator who makes a binding decision.

Australia has judges that specialise in IP disputes and cases are heard in federal courts. There is also the Copyright Tribunal. In China, the Supreme People's Court has judges that specialise in IP. In Indonesia commercial courts hear business disputes including IP cases. In Singapore some IP cases can be brought before their High Court.

> **INNOVATION AND OPERATIONS**
> In 2012 there were over 20,000 trademark applications in Australia under the Madrid Protocol and another 20,000 made in individual countries.

Product liability

Globalisation offers opportunities for Australian businesses to expand into new markets, find new business partners and suppliers. It also creates significant operational and regulatory challenges around product liability. Operating in different countries with different laws and regulations makes managing product liability risk complex.

Laws of countries hold the business responsible for any loss, damage or injury caused by any product. Legal liability travels with every product that is exported and sold overseas. Global consumers are aware of their rights and will exercise those rights by filing product liability suits against exporters, manufacturers, processors and suppliers of products. When managing product liability the different policies and regulations in all the countries where a business operates must be considered.

Product liability risks include:

- fines and penalties for breaching laws and regulations
- civil damages
- boycotts and negative social media campaigns
- costly court actions
- product recalls
- loss of market share
- loss of sales
- damage to the business' public image in the event of a product failure.

Just one liability claim could put a severe financial strain on a business. Even a business defending itself against a claim and winning can cost millions of dollars in legal costs and public relations.

For example, if a sharp edge or a small removable part was left on a product and a child gets hurt using it, the business will be liable for legal action and civil damages.

A business can be held liable for a faulty or dangerous product in one of three ways:

- **Negligence:** a business fails to take reasonable care to manufacture, supply and sell a safe product or provide adequate warnings and instructions.
- **Strict liability:** harm or injury is caused by using the product.
- **Breach of warranty:** the does not meet the legal requirement of being fit and suitable for its purpose.

Product liability insurance protects you in case a product causes harm to a customer, their property or the environment. Insurance is recommended for every business that manufactures a product.

The level of insurance required depends on:

- how likely it is for the product to cause harm
- the severity of the harm that it could cause.

If the product has a high risk of injury, insurance cover must be higher. Liability in products can include design defects and manufacturing defects. Harm or injury may also be caused by inadequate labelling, poor instructions for use or the absence of warnings about the product ingredients, use or storage.

Product liability insurance does not prevent a product from failing or causing harm. If a product fails, a business can make a claim and use the insurance payout to help pay the legal and operational costs of managing the problem.

BUSINESS IN SOCIETY

The Therapeutic Goods Association (TGA) imposed a six-month suspension on Cereform silicone gel-filled breast implants. Since 2009 about 4800 of the implants were sold in Australia. The action prevents the devices from being supplied to the Australian market.

In 2009 there was a product recall of Bonsoy soy milk due to allegations of unusually high levels of iodine in the milk. There was a class action against the Australian distributor of the soy milk on behalf of consumers who alleged injury from consuming the product in the previous five years. A settlement was reached of $25 million to cover legal costs and distribution to the consumers who were part of the class action.

Technological factors

E-commerce is the use of online systems and technologies to conduct business. When launching a global product using e-commerce it is important to design a website that attracts consumers around the world. The design must be stable and able to be accessed with a range of computer operating systems and Internet speeds. Websites designed with language options and for mobile devices are also effective tools for ease of access and purchasing.

It's important to include a payment process for international buyers that is easy to use, secure and which minimises the risk of online fraud. The process must also be designed to collect information from international (and domestic) customers and transactions to refine your marketing strategies.

YouTube
What is e-commerce? (Simple!)

The e-commerce platform can be designed to automatically detect where visitors are in the world and trigger adjustments to website content such as language, currency, prices, shipping information and product availability.

Social media, mobile payments and augmented reality offer new ways to market products and services to consumers. Consumer access to infinite product and service knowledge and globalisation creates business opportunities. But this also increases competition and maintaining an online business and a high level of consumer awareness of online offerings is very costly. Both of which combine to put pressure on profitability.

Consumers use online technologies to search for what they want from around the world; they easily verify product claims through online research and user reviews; and are more difficult to reach through traditional media such as TV and print. Businesses adapt and find new ways to attract and stay connected to customers. Social media is an important tool, but it must be one part of a larger strategy to communicate and attract customers, collect personal information and habits to refine marketing strategies, personalise their experience and make purchasing and payment an easy, trusted process.

Digital distribution

Businesses can reduce the barriers to market entry by distributing their products digitally. They can avoid the cost, risk and time involved in manufacturing and supplying a product, establishing distribution channels (suppliers, wholesalers, retailers) storing and transporting goods into other countries.

Products such as ebooks, music, event tickets, movies, TV shows, software and games can be purchased online then downloaded or streamed instead of objectssuch as discs and packaging being manufactured and delivered to them.

E-commerce security

Customers around the world are more likely to buy products and services online if they are confident that their personal and payment information is secure and their money is going where it should.

Poor ecommerce security is a deterrent for potential e-customers. If security is strengthened consumer confidence will increase and ecommerce will grow. In addition to businesses' security, banks have security measures such as fraud detection and disputed transactions management which also increase consumer confidence in ecommerce.

Secure websites have https not http as part of their website address. Every webpage of an e-commerce website must have https to be secure. A website may have a padlock icon at the bottom of the screen or in the address bar. It indicates that the page uses the SSL protocol.

This is a data transfer security standard that encrypts data and authenticates the server and the integrity of the message. This symbol indicates that all information, most notably banking details, is secured.

To validate customer credit cards businesses can use a payment system that uses live address verification services in the checkout. Fraudulent credit card purchases are prevented by comparing the address entered online to the address on file with the credit card company as part of the transaction process. Another prevention measure is to always request the 3 or 4 digit Card Security Code (CSC) for every online payment.

Businesses can have secure payment processes as part of their shopping cart or use third party services such as Paypal, Visa Checkout or Google Wallet (which may end up being called Android Pay). These have security and fraud management systems in place.

BUSINESS IN SOCIETY

E-commerce in Brazil amounted to over $13 billion in sales in 2013. Brazil ranks 1st in Latin America for credit card fraud. Over 33% of Brazilian credit card users have reported fraudulent activity.

Having a statement or policy about e-commerce security will encourage customers to trust the business. For example, a policy could state that customer information is encrypted, the website is protected by SSL and that credit card details are not stored without consent. There could also be a statement about actions taken if a customer believes there has been fraudulent use of their credit card.

Online criminals illegally access the networks of businesses, steal customer information including credit card details and use it for fraud and identify theft. It is important to have strong security to protect the customer database and business information systems. Security can be strengthened by:

- protecting the business network with a firewall

- using strong encryption for the transmission of data

- not using the default user names and passwords that come with business technology such as Point of Sale systems and software

- keeping anti-malware software up to date and performing frequent virus scans.

E-commerce privacy

Operating an e-commerce web site requires collecting and storing customer details. This includes sensitive information such as address, financial details and other personal information. An important aspect of e-commerce security is the security of customer information.

Businesses have a legal obligation to treat this information carefully and to maintain their privacy. Providing your customers' details to a third party is illegal in most countries and there may be penalties for doing so without consent.

Have a clear privacy policy on the website and clearly state what you will and will not do with customers' personal details and tracking tools such as cookies.

Cookies collect information and send it back to the server of a business. When visiting an e-commerce website cookies are sent to a visitor's computer. It serves as a digital identifier that notifies the vendor whenever that user re-enters the vendor's website. Although an Internet browser can be set to disable cookies, some websites require users to accept them before using the site.

Cookies allow a website to remember a user and what they looked at and used in the site. The website can then automatically customise content and interaction for that user, for example suggested products, currency and shipping information, advertising and promotions. Companies can track a user's cookies around the iInternet and collect information about their surfing habits.

An example of a basic e-commerce Pprivacy statement:

We are committed to protecting the privacy of our customers. We will store customer information securely and not disclose information about our customers to third parties except with your consent orwhen required by law to do so.

YouTube
2014 technology trends: Mobility

Companies operating globally are subject to the privacy laws of each country. The best idea is to have strong privacy policies and systems to ensure compliance with the range of laws they operate under.

In Australia there are the National Privacy Principles (NPPs) detailed in the *Privacy Act 1988*. In China the *Computer Processed Personal Information Protection Act 1995* protects personal information processed by computers.

In New Zealand, the *Privacy Act 1993* sets out principles in relation to the collection, use, disclosure, security and access to personal information.

India does not have comprehensive privacy laws in place. The laws that do exist relate to the privacy of data held by banks. Taiwan has the *Personal Data Protection Act*.

CHAPTER 19
Unit 4 Environment activities

'Because we are a globally connected village,
we need to remember that our choices are not isolated.
They have a powerful ripple effect, and that ripple is global.'
– Linda Fisher Thornton –

Topic study

1. What are the three ways we can understand culture?

2. What are some aspects of cultural values?

3. Why is understanding culture important for business success?

4. List two ethical issues in global business.

5. What are four economic factors that can have an impact on global business?

6. Explain how interest rates can influence economic activity.

7. What is discretionary spending?

8. Explain what happens if the Australian dollar rises against foreign currency.

9. Explain what happens if the Australian dollar falls against foreign currency.

10. List two examples of financial institutions a company could go to for funding.

11. List two examples of external funding for a company.

12. What other factors have an impact on global business?

13. What are three examples of political risk that must be considered when assessing global business growth?

14. What is the WIPO?

15. What are the three ways a business can be held liable for a faulty or dangerous product?

16. What is corporate social responsibility (CSR)?

Business research

1. Economic factors in the global market

This task involves a group research task. There are parts to the task which are to be shared equally.

Write a brief Partnership Agreement to document the contributions and responsibilities of each task group member. Use these headings:

- Date of commencement
- Purpose
- Partners
- Division of work - what topic is each partner reporting on?
- List the specifications of the work – what parts must be completed and documents submitted

i. Individual tasks

Research the following and plan your work with the 4 Plan.

Prepare a written report on the following:

- Law of supply and supply curves
- Law of demand and demand curves
- Equilibrium price and price discovery

ii. Partnership tasks

- Hold a Partnership meeting to discuss your key points
- Work together to develop a presentation that addresses the following:
    - How does inflation influence supply and demand?
    - How could high interest rates and unemployment influence supply and demand?
    - Discuss the likelihood of reaching an Equilibrium Price in a global marketplace.

2. Technological factors

Governments around the world have a vested interest in ensuring customers and businesses can buy and sell online with confidence. Online business offers growth opportunities domestically and for entry into international markets.

i. Discuss how a domestic business could expand globally using technology.

ii. What are two security risks an Australian business could face when using e-commerce internationally.

iii. Discuss Australian laws that regulate ecommerce in Australia and one other country of your choice.

3. Corporate social responsibility

Research Australian companies that operate internationally. Find examples of corporate social responsibility statements or policies. Choose two examples.

i.   For each company list the areas that their CSR policies focus on.

ii. In your opinion are they practical and are their results measurable?

iii. Discuss whether the commitment to CSR would encourage customers to buy their products and services.

iv. Discuss an example of a company that in your opinion is not socially responsible when operating internationally.

Response

1. Impact of technology

Developments in technology have affected the music industry in many ways. Vinyl records were followed by cassette tape and then CDs in the 1980s. The transition to CDs was a bonus to the music industry because consumers replaced their records and cassettes with CDs. Music companies sold millions of CDs without having to invest in new artists and music. The cost to the music companies was small, but profits and sales were high.

Things began to change. CDs were being copied and shared and music files were shared on the Internet.

CD sales started to fall because of file sharing and also because people could now access music in different ways. MP3 players meant that thousands of songs could be stored on devices and mobile phones can access, store and play music files.

Illegal copying of music has been blamed for the downturn in sales. Another cause is the fact that the music industry had been slow to react to the changes in technology and had not appreciated what consumers want from their music.

The Arctic Monkeys made their way in the industry by encouraging fans to put their songs on the Internet. They built up their fan base as people were able to hear the songs and decide whether they liked the band.

Their debut album called *Whatever people say i am, that's what i'm not*, was released in January 2006 and sold 360,000 copies in the first week – the fastest selling debut chart album in UK history.

The Arctic Monkeys embraced new technology to build their fan base rather than try to fight against it. Businesses in the music industry are looking at the success they have had and seeing if they can learn from it.

i.   Discuss four areas of a business that could benefit from new technology.

ii. Apple's iTunes downloading service has been a big success. What might be some of the business reasons for this success?

iii. British music retailer HMV closed stores and sacked staff after a major fall in income and profits. Explain how changes in technology and consumer spending patterns may have caused the financial difficulty.

iv. If you were part of a band like the Arctic Monkeys, what predictions would you make about how the music industry will develop over the next five years? Provide the reasoning behind your answer.

2. Economic factors in the global market

In July 2015 the Australian dollar went below US$0.75 and was predicted to fall below US$0.70 with a real risk of US$0.60 over the next year.

i. Discuss the impact of a falling Australian dollar on Australian businesses that operate internationally.

ii. What effect would a falling AUD have on imports and exports?

iii. Discuss whether a rising Australian dollar is good or bad for Australian companies operating globally.

3. Political factors in the global market

International investors look to sovereign risk as a vital factor when allocating their investments around the world. One measure of risk is a country's sovereign credit rating. Since 2011, Australia has had a triple-A rating from credit ratings agencies; Moody's, Standard and Poor's, and Fitch.

i. Explain what is meant by the term sovereign risk.

ii. Why is it an important consideration for international companies?

iii. List the top five best countries based on sovereign risk.

iv. Discuss how political instability and civil unrest could affect global business.

CHAPTER 20
Strategic management

'With a clever strategy, each action is self-reinforcing.
Each action creates more options that are mutually beneficial.
Each victory is not just for today but for tomorrow.'
– Max McKeown –

STRATEGIC MANAGEMENT

A strategic plan outlines a company's direction and priorities. The plan guides management when they are making decisions about the allocation of resources and assets. The strategic planning process involves stakeholders of the company and its purpose is to build commitment to the agreed upon goals and objectives.

There are five elements in the strategic planning process.

SITUATION ANALYSIS	The external and internal environments are assessed. Strengths and weaknesses, opportunities and threats are identified. The business sets a starting point, 'this is where we are'. It is conducted on a domestic and global basis. Suitable tools are SWOT and PEST.
MISSION STATEMENT	The mission statement communicates to all stakeholders the core purpose and values of the company. It is the vision the owners and managers have for the business. It can take the form of a vision statement or a statement of corporate philosophy.
GOALS AND OBJECTIVES	Goals are expressions of strategic intent. The SMART process can be used to set goals. Objectives give more detail to the goals. They include the KPIs the business will use to measure progress towards the goals. While goals may be set for the long term, objectives are planned to be achieved in the short and medium term.
STRATEGIES	A strategy is a plan of action to achieve the objectives. Strategies are developed for operations, marketing, competition and expansion. Strategies guide the development of action plans that detail what employees need to do in the short term to implement the strategies and achieve the objectives.
REVIEW	The implementation of the strategies and progress towards the goals are measured with KPIs. Issues are identified and plans are made for any corrective action. This may occur at the end of the timeline set by the strategic planning process. The review includes a situation analysis to respond to changes in the business environment and internally. The strategic planning process starts again.

EXAMPLE

Tourism WA's strategic plan was published in 2008. The strategy details the direction for Tourism WA and the Western Australian tourism industry up to 2013. The global financial crisis had an impact on the tourism industry and the organisation reviewed their strategic plan to respond to the change in the business environment.

MISSION STATEMENT

To develop, promote and protect Western Australia's iconic tourism experiences.

GOALS AND OBJECTIVES

One goal is to improve the quality of visitor experiences to match or exceed consumer expectations. An objective is to increase the percentage of visitors who have or will refer others to WA. The KPI is the percentage of visitors that intend to recommend a holiday in WA to others. If 50% or more of visitors surveyed say they intend to recommend WA the objective has been achieved.

STRATEGIES

Strategies to achieve this goal include consumer research, improving the quality of products and services and using the Internet and social media to create positive word of mouth.

EXAMPLE

The Western Australian Cricket Association's strategic plan covering the period from 2008 to 2011 expresses its vision to create the same excitement for the sport that was seen at its peak in the 1970s.

YouTube
Introduction to strategic management

MISSION STATEMENT

Leading WA cricket back to the top.

GOALS AND OBJECTIVES

There are six goals the Association wants to achieve, including to increase the profile of cricket in WA. Objectives, or performance targets as stated in the plan, include increasing traffic to the WACA's website by 10% each year and increasing crowds and television ratings by 5% each year.

STRATEGIES

Strategies WACA will implement to achieve the objectives include using the customer database to communicate with the target market and improving the presentation and marketing of WACA events.

Mission statement

A business' mission statement outlines its purpose of going into business, what it wants to achieve and how it is different to its competitors.

Key values

Key values identify the foundation for the culture of business. They are the norms and standards that are expected of employees in the way they work and interact with other employees, customers and suppliers.

Environmental scan

Also known as a situational analysis, a scan researches and analyses the business environment to identify and anticipate factors that will affect business growth and success. Without a good scan there will be factors that affect sales, costs and profits that were not anticipated and prepared for. There are various models to use to organise a scan and the information it brings. In this chapter the following models are discussed:

- **PEST**
- **Porter's Five Forces**
- **SWOT analysis**

By understanding the business environment informed decisions can be made about:

- marketing mix
- advertising
- new products and services
- target markets
- compliance with laws and regulations
- obtaining business funding
- recruiting or dismissing staff and assigning shifts and hours.

Remember that the business environment is made up of three layers: macro, operating and internal as shown in Figure 20.I.

Internal
- culture
- employees
- management style
- business form

Operating
- competitors
- customers
- suppliers
- local community

Macro
- laws and regulations
- technology
- economy
- social trends

Figure 20.1: Three business environments

PEST

PEST is a method used to analyse the macro environment of a business. Each of the factors identified in a PEST analysis are examined in terms of their impact on the business and the likelihood of it occurring. The analysis should be ongoing so change and trends can be identified and included when making decisions about the business. PEST is an acronym identifying the four elements of the macro environment as shown in Figure 20.2 on the following page.

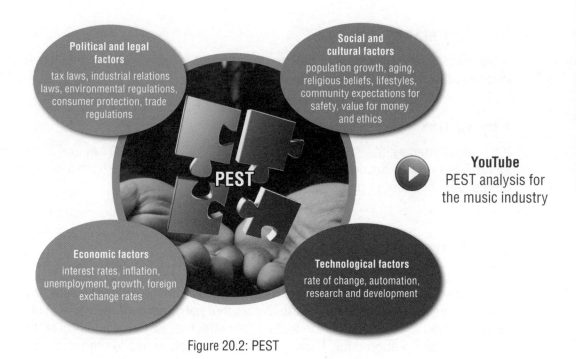

Figure 20.2: PEST

Porter's Five Forces

Porter's Five Forces explains an industry's level of competition. Analysing a market on the basis of the five forces assists management to evaluate the viability of entering a new market or expansion into an existing one. The strength of the forces determines how easy or difficult it is to compete in a market.

New entrants

If it is easy for new businesses to enter a market, competition will increase. If the intellectual property of products is not protected or supplies are easy to obtain then little can stop a competitor from selling the same products to the same people.

Power of suppliers

If one supplier controls the market they can set high prices. If a supplier has little bargaining power, businesses can more easily negotiate lower prices for materials and products. A business may be able to persuade a supplier to sign an exclusive deal with them only, which will prevent other businesses from selling the products.

An example of low supplier power is in the dairy industry. Dairy farms are finding it difficult to survive and large national supermarket companies have been able to negotiate low prices for milk.

Power of buyers

This is how much pressure customers can place on a business. If one customer is large enough and a major source of sales for a business, any change in purchasing they make will have an impact on business survival. This powerful customer may be able to negotiate lower prices and a level of service that leads to a squeeze on profit margins.

Customers with low power will pay whatever prices and accept whatever level of service a business offers.

Availability of substitutes

What is the likelihood that someone will switch to a competitive product or service? If the cost of switching is low, then this poses a serious threat. Below are a few factors that can affect the threat of substitutes.

Level of competition

This describes the intensity of competition between existing firms in an industry. Highly competitive industries generally earn low returns because the cost of competition is high. A highly competitive market might result from a number of forces.

The forces are summarised in the following diagram.

PORTER'S FIVE FORCES

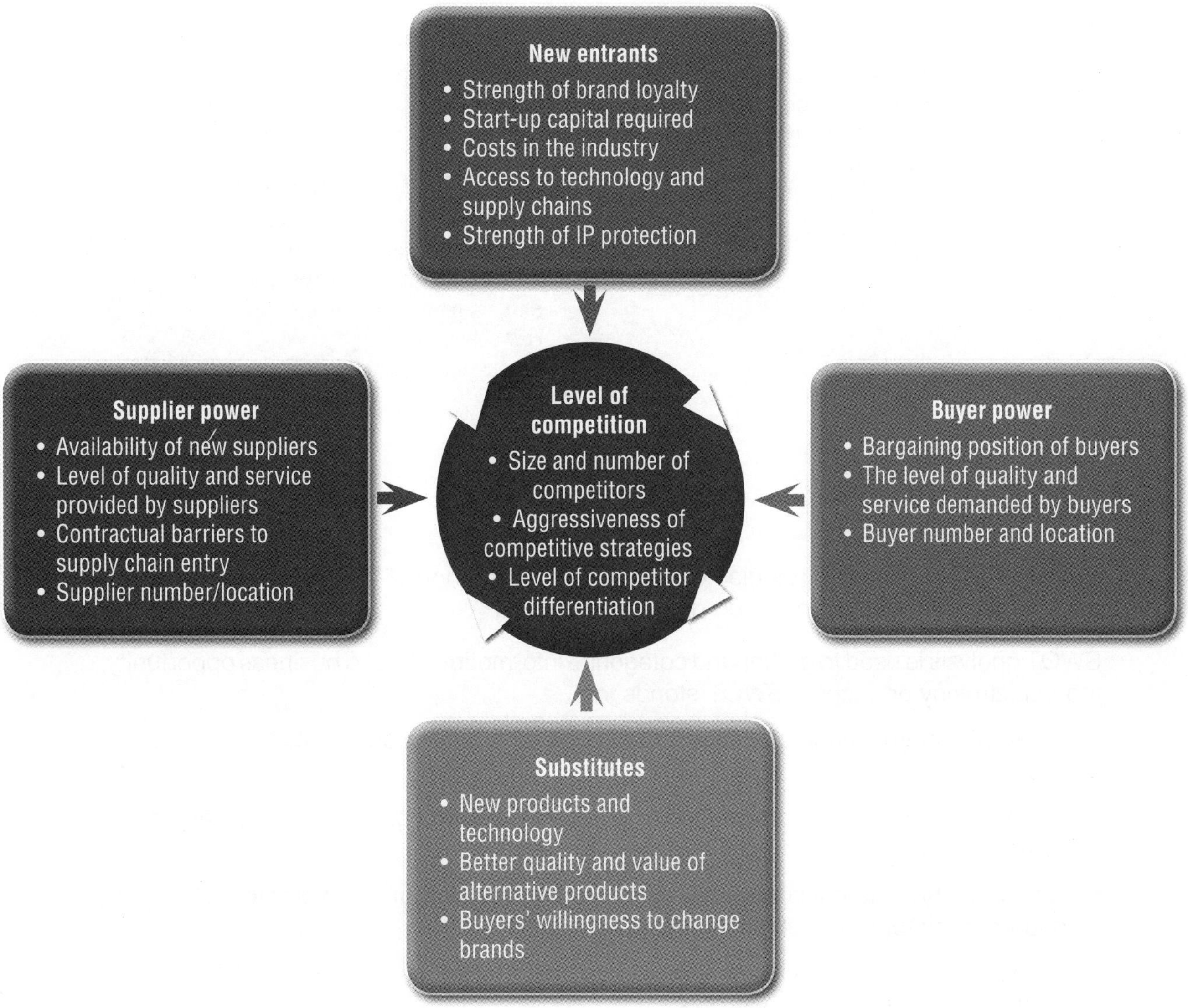

New entrants
- Strength of brand loyalty
- Start-up capital required
- Costs in the industry
- Access to technology and supply chains
- Strength of IP protection

Supplier power
- Availability of new suppliers
- Level of quality and service provided by suppliers
- Contractual barriers to supply chain entry
- Supplier number/location

Level of competition
- Size and number of competitors
- Aggressiveness of competitive strategies
- Level of competitor differentiation

Buyer power
- Bargaining position of buyers
- The level of quality and service demanded by buyers
- Buyer number and location

Substitutes
- New products and technology
- Better quality and value of alternative products
- Buyers' willingness to change brands

Examples

Apple has sustained a competitive advantage due to its unique and innovative products. Apple's first success was its graphic based user interface. It was unique in the industry until Microsoft launched their Windows operating system. Apple's success with their iPod created a new technology market and paved the way for their iTunes Store. A unique product ensured the success of their online media store business model.

Dell's competitive advantage is its pricing of computers. Using Just In Time inventory management means that they are able to maintain low costs. Cost savings from not having to purchase and maintain warehouses of stock waiting to be purchased and a network of shops around the country are passed on to the consumer in their lower prices.

Porter suggests that the five forces determine whether an industry has high profits or low profits. A high profit industry gives a business more control over costs and prices and enables them to capture and keep market share. A low profit industry's competitive pressures keep prices and profits low.

YouTube
Porter's Five Forces
Rubber Duck

LOW PROFITS
- Suppliers with high bargaining power
- Customers with high bargaining power
- Easy entry for competitors
- Many substitutes
- High level of competition

HIGH PROFITS
- Suppliers with little bargaining power
- Customers with low bargaining power
- Barriers preventing competitors
- Few substitutes
- Low competition

SWOT analysis

Business decisions and strategies are influenced by a range of factors that are analysed using a decision-making tool such as SWOT analysis.

SWOT analysis is used to gather and categorise information about a business opportunity, market, strategy or change. SWOT stands for:

- **Strength:** internal characteristics and capabilities that can contribute to business success.

- **Weakness:** internal characteristics and weaknesses that could cause barriers to business success.

- **Opportunity:** external conditions, events and changes that could create opportunities for a business to succeed and grow.

- **Threat:** external conditions, events and changes that could have a negative impact on a business and how it operates.

SWOT analysis is a planning tool that is effective at evaluating the current state of a business. It explores the business's internal and external capabilities showing its position in relation to achieving the business goals. The strengths and weaknesses of a business will determine how well it can respond to and exploit opportunities and threats.

Things to consider when conducting a SWOT include:

- a company's strengths and its weaknesses
- products and/or services and their strengths and weaknesses
- the surrounding community
- target markets
- the competition
- external forces that will affect the business
- opportunities that are available or anticipated
- environmental, technological and social factors
- current or anticipated changes to laws and regulations.

YouTube
McDonalds SWOT

The effectiveness of SWOT analysis depends on the quality of information that is gathered internally and externally. It may be difficult to collect good information from primary sources about markets and communities in other countries.

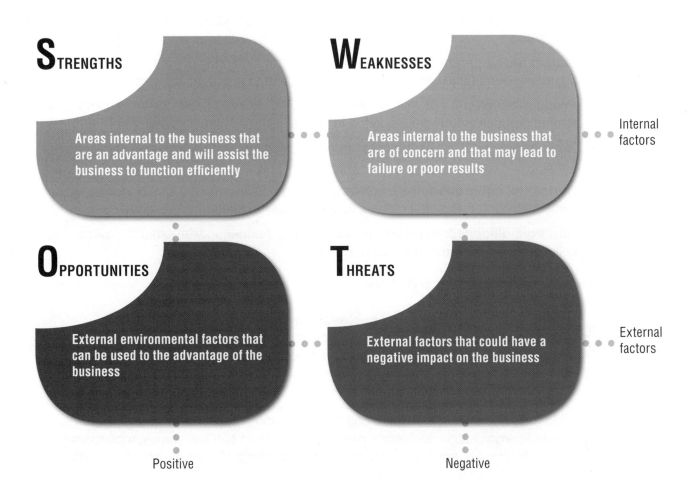

STRENGTHS

Areas internal to the business that are an advantage and will assist the business to function efficiently

WEAKNESSES

Areas internal to the business that are of concern and that may lead to failure or poor results

Internal factors

OPPORTUNITIES

External environmental factors that can be used to the advantage of the business

THREATS

External factors that could have a negative impact on the business

External factors

Positive   Negative

Strategic planning

Scanning the macro environment and using tools to analyse the market and possible business opportunities is part of the process to develop long-term strategies for the business.

Strategic planning consists of the following stages.

Strategic formulation

Strategies are aimed at improving business performance and profits. They focus is on how the business can gain a competitive advantage and succeed in the market.

From these general strategies, managers develop more specific business strategies which provide guidance and direction on achieving the objectives and goals set out in the mission statement. Some examples of strategic goals that can be implemented in a business are:

- **Growth:** also referred to as market penetration, this involves the company focusing its resources on the growth of a particular product in a market.

- **Market development:** this involves modifying the marketing of your current products by adding distribution channels or updating advertising and promotions.

- **Product development:** this involves modifying existing products or creating new related products which are marketed to your existing customers.

- **Innovation:** this involves the creation or modification of new products, services and ideas.

- **Horizontal integration:** this involves acquiring businesses of a similar nature, which eliminates competitors and creates access to new markets.

- **Strategic alliances:** this involves contractually partnering with other businesses to collaborate on particular projects or tasks.

The steps to formulate strategies are:

Analyse the business and business environment
Analyse strengths, weaknesses, opportunities and threats, undertake competitor analysis, identify trends and anticipate changes.

Set a clear strategic direction
Identify key values, a mission and goals including measurable targets for the whole organisation. By clearly defining the mission and key values, management and employees can have a common understanding of what is expected of them and what they are working towards.

Develop projects or initiatives
Outline projects or initiatives at the department, and middle level of the business. By achieving these projects the long-term strategies will be implemented.

 Establish action plans
These plans are aimed at the team and individual level. By achieving the action plans, projects will be completed.

Strategic implementation

The strategy is more likely to work if it builds on and aligns with existing systems and culture. Everyone within the workplace must understand their responsibilities and how they fit in with the overall goals. This is where resistance to change may arise, employees may not agree with or support the strategy. Overcoming resistance to change is part of successful strategy implementation.

The resources and funding the strategy requires must be organised and allocated. Budgeting for and allocating resources shows commitment to achieving strategic goals and is a big step in making the strategy happen..

Communication

Tell them why. A good way to communicate strategy and develop commitment to it is by explaining the 'why'. Staff will be able understand the benefits to them and the business of the strategy and the risks involved if the strategy is not implemented. They do not have to understand every detail at first but be motivated by what can be achieved.

There should be a communication plan as part of implementing a strategy at company-wide, team and department levels, and at an individual level, using a range of communication methods such as email, meetings, newsletters, strategy documents and videos.

Evaluation and control

Strategy evaluation and control includes performance measurements and regular reviews of operations to identify and make corrective actions. Evaluate progress by comparing results to the planned targets and timeframes.

Monitoring the internal and external environments enables a business to collect information and respond to changes and problems. By responding quickly negative impacts can be controlled.

Evaluation and control follows the cycle as shown here.

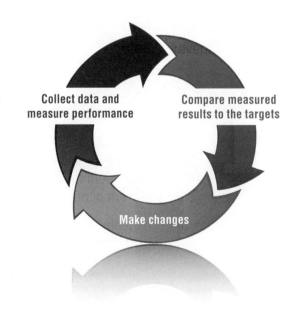

Collect data and measure performance

Compare measured results to the targets

Make changes

Questions to ask when evaluating a strategy include:

- Are the goals and objectives being achieved?
- Are the time frames being met?

- Are the time frames realistic?

- Have there been unanticipated changes, events or market conditions?

- Do staff have adequate resources (money, equipment, facilities, expertise) to achieve the goals?

- What improvements can we make?

- Do we need to revise the goals?

Success should be acknowledged and celebrated. This reinforces the strategic path and the desired values and keeps staff motivated.

CHAPTER 21
Financial indicators

'Long term thinking and planning enhances short term decision making.
Make sure you have a plan of your life in your hand,
and that includes the financial plan and your mission.'
– Manoj Arora –

FINANCIAL RATIOS

Business finances are controlled by planning future income and expenditure and by maintaining accurate records of all cash flows into and out of the business. The actual income and costs are compared to those planned or budgeted for to assess financial performance.

Financial performance of a business is also compared to previous periods, similar businesses and industry performance. This is done using financial ratios, calculated using data from the income statements and balance sheets.

Ratios are indicators of performance and are used to measure business activity. Ratios are compared with those of previous periods of time to monitor and identify trends in business performance. Ratios can also be compared to industry averages and similar businesses to evaluate performance.

Performance targets can be set using ratios. For example, a business wants to achieve a certain profit or rate of return target by the end of the financial year. The viability of business opportunities or targets for acquisition can be assessed in part by their financial ratios.

Financial reporting is more complex when a business is operating internationally. Companies need to collect financial data from a range of countries and regions in different currencies and collate them into consolidated financial statements.

The amounts used in the ratio calculations are taken from the income statement and balance sheet.

Limitations with using ratios

1. Ratios do not explain why, they do not identify the causes of problems.
2. Ratios present limited information and must be viewed in the context of the business and compared to previous periods or industry benchmarks to be meaningful.
3. Comparison with other businesses may be flawed because of different accounting policies.
4. Some figures are based on estimates, for example depreciation, doubtful debts.

When comparing financial ratios between periods it is important to be aware of any changes in the accounts. There may be differences in when income and costs were recognised or different interpretations of accounting standards. There may also be large costs or income items that are the result of a one-off event.

Comparing financial ratios to other companies may also be misleading. Different companies may prepare their accounts and financial reports based on different accounting assumptions.

Types of ratios

Three aspects of business performance are analysed using financial ratios for profitability, liquidity and gearing.

1. Profitability

Profitability indicates the capacity of a business to make profit and provide a return on investment. Figures are taken from the income statement. The ratio for rate of return on owner's equity also uses the shareholders' equity amount from the balance sheet.

A way to improve profitability ratios is by cutting business costs. Reducing costs needs to be managed so customers are not lost through poor service, poor quality or lack of advertising. Reducing costs may lead to a fall in sales which will compound profitability problems. Increasing sales income through advertising or other promotions will also increase costs.

Profitability ratios are summarised in the table below.

Profitability ratio	Formula	Comments
Profit	$\dfrac{\text{Profit}}{\text{Net income}}$ $\dfrac{150\ 000}{720\ 000}$ $= 0.21$	The ratio shows how many cents profit is earned for every dollar of income. The profit ratio can be improved by cutting costs and increasing revenue either by more sales or higher sales prices. For every dollar of sales the business makes 21c profit.

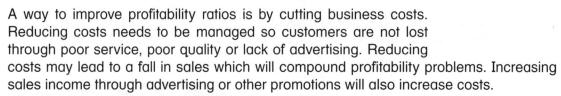

Profitability ratio	Formula	Comments
Gross profit	$\dfrac{\text{Gross profit}}{\text{Net income}}$ $\dfrac{230\,000}{720\,000}$ $= 0.32$	This ratio shows how many cents of gross profit are in each dollar of sales. The gross profit margin can be increased by finding cheaper suppliers for stock and increasing sales prices. For every dollar of sales the business makes 32c of gross profit.
Expenses	$\dfrac{\text{Operating expenses}}{\text{Net income}}$ $\dfrac{160\,000}{720\,000}$ $= 0.22$	This ratio shows the amount of expense in each dollar of income earned. Cost control is needed to improve the expenses ratio. There is 22c of expenses for every dollar of income earned.
Rate of return on owner's equity	$\dfrac{\text{Profit} \times 100}{\text{Shareholders' equity}}$ $\dfrac{560\,000 \times 100}{4\,000\,000}$ $= 14\%$	This ratio shows the return made by the owners on their investment in the business. The ratio shows the percentage return on the owners' investment in the business. The result can be compared to other investments to decide how to invest. Shareholders are receiving a 14% return on their investment in the company.

A high gross profit allows the business to cover expenses and make a reasonable profit. Should there be a reduction in the ratio over a period of time it would indicate the selling price needs to be increased or the cost of sales needs reduction. A low ratio means the business may not be able to cover its expenses and a net loss is likely.

This ratio is important as over a period of time it would indicate the profit trend and whether action needs to be taken to improve the ratio result. A higher value indicates a favourable return on each dollar of sales.

However, reducing costs needs to be finely balanced so that customers are not lost through poor service, poor quality, lack of advertising and a consequent loss of income.

The profitability ratio enables a judgement on how effectively the owner's funds are being used. The owner can compare this rate of return with other forms of investment and also compare the profitability with other similar businesses. An example is presented on the following page.

EXAMPLE

Over the past two years the following financial information was reported in the income statement and balance sheet of a retail business.

	Year 1 ($)	Year 2 ($)
Net sales	320 000	350 000
Cost of sales	208 000	238 000
Gross profit	112 000	112 000
Costs	32 000	43 000
Profit	80 000	70 000
Shareholders' equity	1 000 000	1 000 000

The following ratios were calculated.

	Year 1	Year 2
Gross profit ratio	35%	32%
Profit ratio	25%	20%
Expenses	10%	12%
ROE	8%	7%

Comments

- The profit ratio has decreased due to increased operating costs.
- Costs have increased significantly which has resulted in a fall in profit despite an increase in sales.

Recommendations:

- Management need to look at increasing prices and reducing costs to respond to the fall in profit.
- The management should investigate whether the increase in costs is ongoing or due to isolated events in Year 2.

2. Liquidity or working capital

The working capital ratio shows the relationship of current assets to current liabilities. It measures how much short-term funds the business has to meet its short-term debts. If the working capital ratio is positive, it indicates that the business is more likely to be able pay what it owes. If the working capital ratio is negative, it indicates that the business may not be able to pay its short-term debts. A high working capital ratio indicates more current assets and the likelihood that a business is able to pay its liabilities. A low ratio may mean creditors may not be paid in the short term.

The current ratio can be improved by increasing current assets while stabilising or decreasing current liabilities.

A business could increase their collections from debtors; encourage them to pay their invoices quickly and to pay cash instead of using credit. Spending more on advertising and discounting sale prices may also increase the cash flow into the business. Items are taken from the balance sheet to calculate liquidity ratios.

Liquidity ratio	Formula	Comments
	Current assets Current liabilities	This ratio indicates liquidity by comparing short-term debt with cash in the business. The result is the amount of current assets for every dollar of current liabilities.
Current	$\dfrac{380\ 000}{275\ 000}$ = $1.38	This indicates that for every dollar of short-term debt there is $1.38 of current assets. Current liabilities can be paid off and the business will have money left over to keep operating.

EXAMPLE

	Year 1	Year 2	Year 3
Current assets	$40 000	$32 000	$24 000
Current liabilities	20 000	24 000	28 000

The liquidity ratio for each of the three years:

Liquidity ratio	Year 1	Year 2	Year 3
Current assets Current liabilities	$\dfrac{40\ 000}{20\ 000}$ = 2:1	$\dfrac{32\ 000}{24\ 000}$ = 1.3:1	$\dfrac{24\ 000}{28\ 000}$ = 0.9:1

In Year 1 for every dollar in current liabilities, there was $2.00 in current assets. This indicates that short-term debt could be paid comfortably, leaving working capital to run the business. In Year 2 this figure decreased to $1.30 and in Year 3 to 90c. This indicates a downward trend in liquidity.

3. Stability or gearing

Gearing indicates how reliant on debt a business is for its operating funds. The ratio indicates whether a business has high or low gearing. A business aims for a contribution of 50c debt for every dollar of equity at the most.

If a business is highly geared it relies heavily on borrowed funds to operate (creditors have greater equity in the business than the owners). Debt may provide funds for operation and expansion, but it is also a drain on cash as debt repayments must be met. Creditors may also want to be more involved in the running of the business if there are substantial debts, and may move in to take business assets to recover their money.

If the business is lowly geared it is because the business operates using owner's capital and retained profits more than loans from banks or creditors. This means that the business has lower debt repayments, making it more stable and with lower financial risk.

The gearing ratio can be improved by paying off short-term debt, additional capital from owners or additional share issues. Items for the ratio are taken from the balance sheet.

Gearing ratio	Formula	Comments
	$\dfrac{\text{Total liabilities}}{\text{Equity closing balance}}$	The result is the number of cents of short and long-term debt for every dollar of owner's equity. A business aims for a contribution of 50c debt for every dollar of equity at the most.
Debt to equity	$\dfrac{325\ 000}{195\ 000}$ $= 1.67$	For every dollar contributed by owners there is $1.67 contributed by debt. It shows that the business relies more on debt than equity to finance its operations.

EXAMPLE

	Year 1	Year 2	Year 3
Total liabilities	$80 000	$90 000	$110 000
Equity (at the end)	100 000	100 000	100 000

The debt to equity ratio for each of the three years is as follows:

Debt to equity ratio	Year 1	Year 2	Year 3
$\dfrac{\text{Total liabilities}}{\text{Equity (at the end)}}$	$\dfrac{80\ 000}{100\ 000}$ $= 0.8:1$	$\dfrac{90\ 000}{100\ 000}$ $= 0.9:1$	$\dfrac{110\ 000}{100\ 000}$ $= 1.1:1$

This indicates that in Year 1 the business borrowed 80 cents for every dollar contributed by the owners. In Year 2 the level of borrowing increased to 90c for each dollar contributed by the owners. In Year 3 it increased to $1.10.

This indicates the business is increasingly geared, depending on debt to finance operations. At the end of Year 3, outside sources of finance have more equity in the assets of the business than the owner has. This may make the business less financially stable.

Usually the higher the gearing, the greater the financial risk to the business because of the larger burden of debt repayments. When borrowing increases, the business is under more pressure to generate the cash to make repayments as well as to fund operations and growth. If business is making high income and profits it isn't a problem. If there is an economic downturn, a drop in sales or increase in costs, the business might have trouble meeting debt obligations.

It's not necessarily a bad thing for a business to be highly geared. The borrowings could be for expansion, therefore making it possible to earn more revenue and become more profitable.

Being lowly geared may mean the business is unable to expand or fight off competition because funds are limited to retained profits. They may raise capital through share issues but this is a process that takes time and dilutes ownership of the company.

Interpreting ratios

As discussed earlier, analysis of ratios must be done in the context of the whole business, past performance and the performance of similar businesses and the industry. Looking at ratios over time will reveal trends that can be investigated further. Ratios can highlight areas of the business, such as debt or costs, that need attention.

When assessing financial ratios, the following questions are important:

- What does a change in the ratio mean?
- What is the industry benchmark or average?
- What are the limitations of the ratio?
- What external factors are having an impact on the ratio?
- Is it because of an isolated event or a trend?

YouTube
3 Minutes! Financial ratios and financial ratio analysis

CHAPTER 22
Product management

'If advertisers spent the same amount of money on improving
their products as they do on advertising then they
wouldn't have to advertise them.'

– Will Rogers –

Production refers to the methods and processes involved in building a product. The
production concept states that:

*If we can build quality products at affordable prices,
minimise costs and keep quality high
the products will sell themselves*

PRODUCTION MANAGEMENT SYSTEMS

The process of production is also known as the 'transformation process'. It takes raw
materials, skills, knowledge and technology and transforms them into a finished
product. If the selling price for the finished product is greater than the total cost of
production, the business has added value and will make a profit.

The production process can be viewed as a system with inputs that are processed into
outputs:

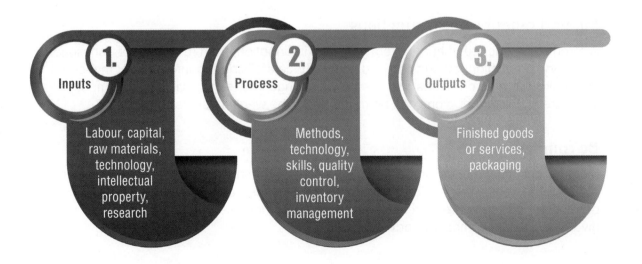

1. Inputs	2. Process	3. Outputs
Labour, capital, raw materials, technology, intellectual property, research	Methods, technology, skills, quality control, inventory management	Finished goods or services, packaging

Production management systems work to monitor and control the production process to ensure the inputs are organised, production processes are operating effectively and efficiently, and the outputs meet quality standards and client needs.

Production management systems are linked to sales, inventory and customer systems to help a business plan production schedules and materials purchasing. Production targets are set based on customer orders or inventory levels and the production management system is used to gather production, inventory and customer data to ensure the targets are reached.

The goal of production management is to produce goods and services at the right quality, right quantity, at the right time and at minimum cost. If achieved a business can compete effectively in the marketplace. A production management system ensures that a business gets the most out of their production capability.

A good production management system helps a business to attain the following.

Achieve business goals

Production management helps a business to produce products that meet customer needs at an affordable price at minimised costs. This will increase its sales and generate profit.

Build a positive public image

If customers are receiving high quality products that are not faulty, on demand at an affordable price they will be happy. Happy customers tell other people about the business and come back to the business to buy again. This builds a good reputation and public image that results in long-term success.

Support other business functions

A production management system collects information from a range of functions, inventory, production, purchasing and sales. By centralising the information, managers can make informed decisions and see how a change in one area will have an impact on other areas. Better decisions can be made about the whole business.

Be competitive

Meeting customer needs and keeping them happy, minimising costs and increasing sales will increase profit. More income in the business can be used for advertising, promotion and market research. These factors will increase competitiveness and may give a business a competitive advantage.

YouTube
Production manager

PRODUCT DEVELOPMENT

Product development can be based on incremental innovation or disruptive innovation.

INCREMENTAL INNOVATION
- Making improvements to existing processes, products or services to prolong product life cycle or maintain competitive advantage
- Longer battery life, better quality, software updates, better performance, automated production, Gorilla glass

DISRUPTIVE INNOVATION
- Creating a new process, service or product in response to a market need or opportunity or to create a new market
- Cloud computing, e-commerce, digital radio, 3D printing, driverless cars, wearable technology

Incremental innovation leads to product improvements, new features or better performance. The development adds on to an existing product and customers are still very familiar with it and the brand.

Disruptive innovation results in a totally new product that will be sold to a new or niche market.

Product development involves investing time, money and skills and involves a high level risk. After this substantial investment, customers may not respond to the product. It is important that any product development is based on:

- a clear plan
- market research
- business environment research
- the skills and expertise of staff
- intellectual property protection.

Planning product development and making informed decisions increases the likelihood of success. Product development helps to create new opportunities, increase profits and increase the satisfaction levels of consumers.

Examples of product development include:

- turning a USB storage device into a portable MP3 player
- developing simple mobile phones into smartphones
- building touch screens and tablets to increase the portability of computers
- creating ebooks and distributing them online
- smart and touch screen televisions
- hybrid cars.

INNOVATION AND OPERATIONS

In 1998 Pets.com was launched with a multimillion dollar advertising campaign. The site sold pet food and pet accessories online. The business bought huge warehouses and filled them with stock, waiting for the all the customers they expected. Within two years the business closed. They did not do any market research. If they did they would have found that customers prefer to buy their pet products at the supermarket instead of online and having to wait a few days for delivery. And instead of the expected large orders, customers buy pet food in small amounts as they need it.

Stages in product development

A planned process will increase the likelihood of success when developing a new product or improvements to existing products.

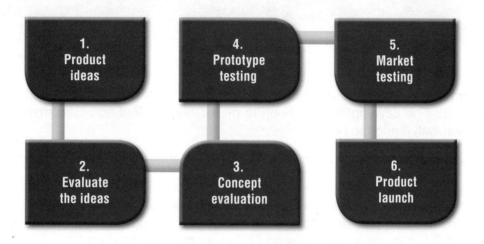

1. Product ideas

Research existing customers, target markets, technology and competitors. Use this information to identify an opportunity for a niche market, an unmet customer need or a way to use value and quality to capture market share. Ask employees for product ideas and survey customers for feedback on existing products.

2. Evaluate the ideas

Make a list of possible product ideas and evaluate them with business leadership or a product development team. It is a good idea to evaluate ideas with people from a range of functions in the business, such as production, sales, marketing and finance. Each idea can then be evaluated in terms of its marketing potential, whether the business is able to produce it efficiently, if there is time and money to do it and if staff are able to sell it. Look at the expected sales, costs and profit for each idea. Discuss the pros and cons and select the best idea.

3. Product concept evaluation

More details are added to the idea, such as possible target markets, designs, colours and name. Seek feedback from customers and employees on the idea. Run focus groups to gather feedback about the idea, possible product names and advertising strategy. Analyse the market to identify competitors selling or developing similar products and if there are any substitutes.

4. Prototype testing

Once the best idea is chosen and tested it can be developed into a prototype. Staff analyse and test the product and give feedback. What people like can be used for advertising and promotions and criticism can be addressed through improvements to the prototype.

5. Market testing

When the prototype is refined market testing can be carried out. A small amount of the product is manufactured. Samples can be distributed to customers on the database or through newspapers, magazines and online registration. Market testing is often a part of the campaign to increase interest and desire before a full product launch.

6. Launch the product

Have inventory ready for customer orders and distribution to retailers. Use a range of promotional strategies to generate interest, desire and demand for the product. New products may need a more extensive strategy because customers will need to be educated and persuaded about a new, unfamiliar product and its benefits.

YouTube
Synapse presents: The product development process

Intellectual property protection

When a business develops a new product it is important to protect the intellectual property (IP) behind it. This will prevent competitors from developing copies and taking market share. If copies are found in the marketplace, a business must take action to enforce their IP rights.

A patent is a useful protection for new products. A patent gives a business a legally enforceable right to manufacture and sell a certain product and prevent other businesses from selling the same and similar products. A patent may not be granted if people are already aware of and have used the new product. It is a good idea to patent the product before developing and testing a prototype and get customers and staff to sign confidentiality agreements before testing the product.

Licensing is another form of protection. It involves an contractual agreement for another company to use the intellectual property you own. They can use it under strict conditions and in return for payment such as an ongoing royalty or a percentage of income.

CHAPTER 23
Process control

> 'The first rule of any technology used in a business is that automation applied to an efficient operation will magnify the efficiency. The second is that automation applied to an inefficient operation will magnify the inefficiency.'
> – Bill Gates –

PROCESS CONTROL

Businesses have processes that result in products being made, services being delivered and customer needs being met. These processes must be free from errors and be relied upon to produce a high quality output consistently.

A business must monitor and review its processes to identify problems and make improvements so customers receive what they ordered without delay. Two ways businesses achieve this is through quality management and inventory control techniques.

Quality management

Quality management refers to ensuring that processes and systems result in a consistently high quality output. A quality product will attract customers and build a positive public image and customer loyalty, ensuring customers will return to the business to buy again.

Quality management is concerned with detecting and removing flaws in systems to prevent products that fall below set quality standards.

Examples

In response to car faults and recalls, Toyota increased their quality control measures using additional engineers called chief quality officers.

The Australian beef industry has the following quality control measures developed and enforced by Meat and Livestock Australia Ltd:

- quality standards for the beef industry
- audits against industry standards and codes of practice
- training programs for operatives working in Industry Accreditation programs
- advice to assist businesses when they are developing quality systems
- distribution of publications covering all aspects of livestock and meat quality.

A pipeline construction company hires welding quality inspectors to inspect welds. After sections of a pipeline are welded together the welds are inspected to make sure they meet quality standards for thickness and consistency. The inspection is carried out by sight and with an X-ray or ultrasound of each weld.

The benefits of quality management

YouTube
Quality management
in 3 Minutes

Quality management is used to isolate and provide feedback on the causes of quality problems. By using this approach, data and feedback work towards identifying root-cause problems and then developing strategies to fix these problems and make improvements.

Quality management can lead to:

- high levels of customer satisfaction
- motivated staff that enjoy working in a workplace committed to doing its best
- reduction of waste by anticipating problems and avoiding time and money spent on fixing errors and defects
- more sales and higher profits because of cost reductions and increased sales
- positive public image built on high quality products and services delivered on time.

Quality management is based on:

- control
- assurance
- improvement.

Quality control (QC) is comparing the results to the plan. It ensures that a manufactured product or a service meets a defined set of quality criteria and the requirements of the customer. The purpose is to identify where the criteria is not being met to put corrective actions in place.

Customer complaints mainly arise because quality has fallen; therefore the objective of QC is realised by keeping quality of output at the right level. Loss of profitability can also occur when products do not comply with local or national regulations; QC can give protection here also. Maintenance of quality is particularly important for branded products, because a brand name becomes associated with a particular quality level, and any lowering of the level causes the customer to lose confidence in the brand; sales of other goods under the same brand may then also be reduced.

The level of QC depends on the size of the company and the kind of products it is manufacturing or delivering. A small assembly plant may carry out QC by inspecting individual parts as the staff assemble them into the finished product. A large manufacturer that may be using a combination of automation and employees will need sophisticated QC. If the product is medical, for human consumption or hazardous such as pharmaceuticals, food, toys or chemicals there would be very strict control with testing at all stages.

QC occurs at four stages:

1. Specifications

If the criteria and requirements for a product are clear and agreed to it will be easier to meet them. It may involve meetings with clients or relevant staff, making designs and

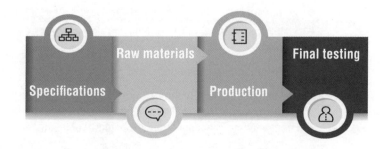

Specifications — Raw materials — Production — Final testing

developing a clear design brief that covers all aspects of a product or service. Quality specifications include appearance, packaging, size, weight, colours and other aspects such as power source, battery life and durability.

2. Raw materials

High quality raw materials must be used to produce high quality products. This can be difficult to manage because there are cost pressures. High quality raw materials are also more expensive so there must be a balance between quality and profitability.

Companies often have quality criteria for raw materials and a preferred supplier list. A company may have trusted suppliers that have their own strict quality controls in place. The company knows that raw materials from these suppliers will meet their own quality specifications.

A basic check is to compare the materials delivered to the purchaser. For example, are the materials what was ordered, are the quantities correct, are they in good condition, have they been damaged in transit? Once the delivery has been accepted the materials can be checked for quality before entering the production process.

QC of raw materials before going into the production process can be difficult to manage. Defects or substandard materials may be found. To return the materials to the supplier and organise replacements or to find a new supplier involves time, delaying production, and may lead to increased costs. There may be pressure to just use the substandard materials to avoid missing deadlines and profit margins. This involves an argument between quality and efficiency. If the substandard materials are used, it might mean production can continue, but the final product will not meet quality specifications which can have an impact on sales and company reputation.

Feedforward controls involve careful planning before production begins. In this way any problems can be anticipated and the solutions prepared. An example of this is a bakery using a recipe and making sure that all ingredients and equipment are clean, suitable and of high quality before making the bread.

3. Production

There are quality control at points in the production process. Operation checks ensure that production machinery and equipment are working as it should. This may involve automated technology such as temperature, speed and defect measurements. Employees may also monitor how plant and equipment is operating and make adjustments as needed. In addition to operation checks there are quality checks during production. Again these are a combination of automation and human checks.

Quality control involves checking the quality of the product at different stages of the production process. Control employs feedforward, concurrent and feedback controls to monitor the production process.

Concurrent controls are used during the production process. An example is the baker checking on the bread during the baking to see if the bread is rising. A production line may scan products with magnets to detect metal in products, or samples may be taken for testing. There may be automated cameras or employees visually inspecting products as they pass through a production line. If problems or defects are found, defective products can be discarded or improvements made to the production process to fix the problem.

4. Final testing

This involves checking the finished product to make sure it meets customer and quality specifications.

Feedback controls occur after the production process. It can involve testing the final product, a final quality checklist before delivery or collecting customer feedback.

In an IT business quality control involves verifying the output conforms to the required specifications. The IT product (database, software, animation, etc.) is checked against customer requirements, with testing and code inspections to ensure that it meets the agreed requirements. Before handover it will be tested to ensure it runs smoothly under different conditions.

There may also be conflict between quality and efficiency at this stage. Rejected products are costly because money has been spent to make them, but they cannot be sold.

Assurance

Quality assurance (QA) establishes a set of procedures or a process so errors are less likely to happen. It is the overall process of managing quality: not just procedures and technology, but also building a culture within the workplace so that every employee works to quality targets and standards.

In designing websites there are quality standards that must be met to ensure the design is right. These standards can be applied to all website projects as part of quality assurance. For example, the websites must work with a variety of web browsers, computers and mobile devices, provide adequate colour contrasts for people with vision difficulties and contain correct spelling and grammar. These standards form the quality criteria that are then applied through quality control.

QA planning is undertaken at the beginning of a project or manufacturing process. The typical outcomes of the QA planning activities are quality plans, inspection and test plans, the selection of defect tracking tools and the training of people in the selected methods and processes.

The purpose of QA is to prevent defects in the first place; QA is proactive.

Undertaking QA at the beginning of a project can reduce the risks that have been identified during the specifications stage. Possible quality issues are identified. QA will include controls that will prevent the quality issues or detect them so they can be fixed.

Improvement

Businesses look to continuous improvement in their production processes as this will result in products and service of higher quality, customer loyalty and attracting new customers through word of mouth and company reputation.

Improvements are aimed at streamlining processes so that waste is eliminated, improving product quality and maximising the skills of the workforce.

A company must have a baseline to compare against. This includes the level of quality that was produced in the past. Improvement is made if the quality is increased compared to past production.

The goals of quality management is to:

- meet required standards
- make improvements to increase quality.

A company can build competitive advantage if they improve their quality to be better than their competitors.

Once again there may be conflict between improving quality and making profit. Improving quality may involve the costs of replacing or upgrading equipment, training staff or bringing in new technology such as automated detection and inspection. The costs in the short term must result in long-term advantage. A business case should be made to demonstrate the benefits from making improvements and the risks if the improvements are not made.

PLAN DO CHECK ACT

A common approach to improving business processes is the Plan Do Check Act cycle.

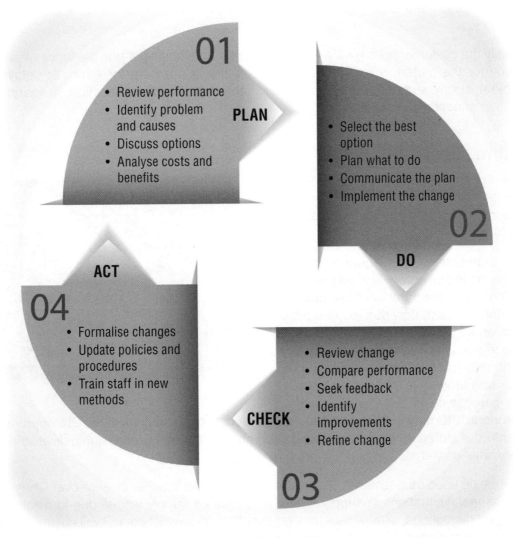

YouTube
Plan Do Check Act fishing

Inventory control

Inventory management encompasses the control of three types of inventory:

- **Materials:** raw materials and other supplies for manufacturing a product.
- **Work in process:** partially completed goods.
- **Finished goods:** the completed products ready for sale to customers.

Two examples of inventory control techniques are Just in time and Just in case.

Just in time

If a business uses just in time (JIT) management they do not maintain an inventory of materials or finished products. When a customer places an order the business then orders materials and manufactures or sources the product and delivers it to the customer. The success of this method relies upon a high level of coordination, reliable suppliers and a highly efficient production process. The JIT inventory method results in low inventory costs because there is no need for a warehouse, warehouse staff and bulk purchases of inventory.

Usually the customer pays for the goods up front so the business has the funds available to pay for the materials and production. But there is no room for errors or delays. A problem at any stage of the supply chain (materials supply, production, delivery) will result in unhappy customers.

Just in case

Just in case (JIC) control is where a business stores and maintains a large amount of inventory to avoid running out of stock.

This approach involves higher costs initially as the inventory is stockpiled, but it reduces the number of lost sales and delay in cash flow due to not having stock on hand. It means that customer service does not depend on suppliers and distributors; delays between a customer order and delivery is minimised. It can also increase costs in terms of storage overheads. JIC may also reduce the transport costs associated with the JIT approach. Inventory is stored in the business and does not have to be ordered and delivered every time, as with JIT.

JIC may be used as a temporary measure to respond to supplier closure over Christmas or seasonal fluctuations in supply. There may also be supply issues due to weather or transport disruptions, or suppliers may go out of business. JIC control will ensure there is stock in the business during these times of uncertainty of supply. A business being able to take an order and deliver a product quickly will differentiate them from their competitors.

JIT or JIC?

The best inventory control technique depends on the business and the stock it needs. A business may also use a combination of techniques to ensure supply and customer service. Factors to consider when deciding on the technique include the following.

Location

If suppliers are local and delivery is quick then JIT will work well. This means that orders will be delivered sooner and there is less chance of delays and damage in transit and lower transport costs. If suppliers are located further away, interstate or overseas, JIC will be a better approach.

Suppliers

If a supplier maintains good inventory and is organised, they can deliver orders quickly so JIT will work. If a supplier needs a long lead time and is less reliable then JIC is better.

Sales forecasting

A combination of JIT and JIC may be best if a business has predictable sales fluctuations, for example seasonal peaks and lows. It may use JIT during low times and JIC during peak periods.

Inventory control system

JIT inventory control requires a sophisticated system to track inventory levels in real time and to identify stock items that need ordering. It may also include automated orders when levels reach a certain point. There may be automated links between the sales and inventory systems to make a stock order once a sale is processed. A business that has a basic system that cannot cope with a JIT approach is more likely to use the JIC technique.

Products

Products like fresh food cannot be stored for long periods and clothing changes seasonally and according to fickle customer tastes. A business will use JIT control to be adaptable and to ensure a fresh supply to customers. JIC is better for stable products and materials that don't perish or go out of fashion.

CHAPTER 24
Technology for global business

'Because we are a globally connected village, we need to
remember that our choices are not isolated.
They have a powerful ripple effect, and that ripple is global.'
– Linda Fisher Thornton –

TECHNOLOGY FOR GLOBAL BUSINESS

As technology adoption rises across Australia, your customers' expectations of your business will increase. Your customers will demand high-quality communication through the Internet and social media. Customers will also expect engaging content and online experiences, as well as innovative mobile commerce tools and applications.

Distribution of products

It is time-consuming and expensive to establish a distribution network domestically. It is more complex to establish one internationally. You will need to deal with different languages, different workplace cultures, different currencies and different postal and transport systems. It will take time to find suitable retailers and find cost-effective ways to either store products in the target country, or distribute products safely and quickly, or a combination.

Technology can assist businesses to get their products to international customers. Instead of having a network of retail stores or agreements with shops to stock your products, customers could buy direct from your website. An Australian business can communicate directly with customers around the world instead of having to go through a network of wholesalers and retailers.

The digital distribution of products will also save time and money, for example software, games, books, tickets and music.

Technology can also be used to help keep track of inventory and automate distribution. An order through a website can be linked to the warehouse for real time stock availability and an order is generated automatically.

> **INNOVATION AND OPERATIONS**
> At Wal-Mart as soon as a customer picks an item of the shelf and the cashier scans it, a signal is sent to the supplier of the product wherever they are in the world. The signal is received by the supplier and the supplier packs the item and ships it to the Wal-Mart store that sold the item. Using this technology in the supply chain, Wal-Mart moves 2.3 billion stock items worldwide each year.

Tracking

Tracking is important for the online business and the customer. If it is easy to track a package, customers will feel more confident to buy from a business. Tracking may involve an additional cost which can be passed on to the customer as part of the delivery charge or as an optional extra.

E-commerce for global growth

A country's potential for online retail success relies on how many people use the Internet and how comfortable they are purchasing products online. The longer a country has had easy access to the Internet the more likely a majority of the population has experience with online shopping and confidence in online payment systems.

BUSINESS IN SOCIETY

The US, UK, Germany, France, Australia and Korea lead the world in Internet use, all with around 80% of their population being Internet users.

Currencies

It is more inviting and less confusing for customers to see prices in their local currency. Online sellers should include the option for customers to customise the website to their chosen currency.

Local payment

Use online payment systems that are familiar to customers and easy for them to access. For example, in Germany wire transfers are the most common payment method and in Japan the konbini payment method is often used for online purchases.

Konbini is a shortened version of the Japanese word for 'convenience store' or small supermarket. A customer orders a product on a website and receives a unique payment number. They take their payment number to a konbini. The customer pays the cash to the store staff and receives a receipt. They then enter the payment number, receipt number and their phone number into a self service terminal in the store. This registers payment with the online seller.

BUSINESS IN SOCIETY

A design principle for websites in Australia is to use space, reduce clutter and to be clear and concise. In China, websites are very content heavy with lots of links and information. Chinese consumers will be attracted to websites that fill the page.

Social media

The term 'social media' is thrown around a lot today and understanding how to integrate social media strategies into your company's promotional activities can be time-consuming, costly and is no guarantee of success.

Social media can be an effective tool to help promote your product or service, but posting photos and links from other sites is not enough to build a presence that keeps customers coming back.

High quality content as part of your social media strategy can turn a website or web presence into a magnet for potential customers.

BUSINESS IN SOCIETY

Globally Facebook has over 1 billion monthly active users. In April 2015 there were 14 million Facebook users and about 3 million Twitter users in Australia. Facebook remains the largest and most used social network. Instagram is continuing to grow with 5 million monthly active users in Australia. Instagram now overtakes Tumblr as the 4th most popular social network in Australia.

YouTube
What is social media?
Find out exactly

Social media engages with customers like traditional media does not. There is a sharing of information, the ability to communicate.

Key social media strategies

Key social media strategies include:

- Create a strategy that integrates content marketing and social media to build relationships with your customers.
- Use social media to respond quickly to questions your customers ask.
- Use social media channels to promote and build engagement and keep customers coming back.

BUSINESS IN SOCIETY

In China, Facebook, YouTube and Twitter are banned but they have local equivalents; Youku, Weibo and Renren.

Blogging

Incorporate content marketing into your communication and promotional strategy. Blogging is the fastest and most efficient way to gain visibility for your brand, product or service. Offer fresh content on company blogs. Having active social media and blogs means that the business, products and brands will rank higher in search engine results.

- Create a realistic schedule and stick to it.
- Align social media and blog posts to current and future marketing strategies.
- Create a content calendar to plan possible future topics and set deadlines for posts.

YouTube
Blogging is critical for business growth

The cloud

Cloud computing means storing and accessing data and programs over the Internet instead of on the business' server. The cloud is just a metaphor for the Internet. It is one way to increase capacity or add capabilities as you need them without investing in new infrastructure, training new staff or licensing new software.

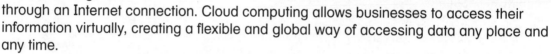

Using the cloud means storing and accessing data and software through an Internet connection. Cloud computing allows businesses to access their information virtually, creating a flexible and global way of accessing data any place and any time.

Cloud computing service providers are often located outside Australia. Before committing, you should investigate where your data is being stored and which privacy and security laws will apply to the data.

Benefits of using the cloud

Scalability

If there are peaks and troughs, seasonal cycles or sudden growth in a business it can quickly and cost-effectively adapt their IT needs using cloud services. Cloud plans can be easily changed to increase or reduce storage space and data access.

If a business provides its own IT services it would have to plan and budget for the cost and space required for new servers, computers and software.

Collaboration

Collaboration in a global business is supported by the cloud. Business information and systems are stored in a central place that can be accessed from anywhere in the world. If you are working on a project across different locations, you could use cloud computing to give employees and contractors access to the same files. Once data is in the cloud, sharing files can be as easy as sending a link, eliminating the process of emailing large files or saving copies on drives that are then mailed.

Flexibility of work practices

Cloud computing allows employees to have the ability to access data from home, when travelling to other locations, in different time zones and out of normal business hours.

Security and data protection

Cloud service providers have backups and security as part of their plans.

 YouTube
Computer basics: What is the Cloud?

CHAPTER 25
Unit 4 Management activities

'Because we are a globally connected village, we need to remember that our choices are not isolated. They have a powerful ripple effect, and that ripple is global.'
– Linda Fisher Thornton –

Topic study

1. List the first two elements of a strategic plan.
2. What is PEST?
3. List Porter's five forces.
4. What are two conditions that result in low profits?
5. What are two conditions that result in high profits?
6. What is analysed with SWOT?
7. Explain two limitations with using financial ratios.
8. What three aspects of business performance can be analysed using ratios?
9. What does 'lowly geared' mean?
10. What are the four things a good production management system helps a business to do?
11. What is the difference between incremental and disruptive innovation?
12. What are the stages in product development?
13. What is quality management?
14. What are the three aspects of quality management?
15. What is the difference between Just in time and Just in case?
16. How can technology assist companies to distribute products globally?
17. What is one example of a key social media strategy?
18. What is the 'cloud'?

Business research

1. Environmental scan – PEST

Work in a small group to plan a global expansion strategy. The planning stage involves comparing Australia to two possible target countries. The analysis will be conducted using PEST. Research and analyse Australia and two other countries of your choice. Use the 4 Plan to organise your research.

i.   Individually research a country and summarise your findings under the PEST headings.

ii. As a group discuss your analysis and use the PEST information to select the preferred option.

iii. Write down your decision and the reasons why you selected that country.

iv. Discuss challenges the selected country may present for an Australian company.

2. Global technology and innovation

Choose a company and research their use of technology to operate globally. For the company prepare a written report or slideshow that evaluates and includes examples of:

i.   Global branding

ii. Standardisation and adaptation in ecommerce strategy

iii. Online advertising

iv. Social media strategies

v.   Recommendations for innovation in the ecommerce strategy

3. Quality management and technology

Global demand for better quality services and products is increasing. Customers around the world demand assurance that the product or services they purchase will meet their expectations. The emphasis on quality products and services is forcing global industries to adopt internationally recognised quality management systems to stay in business.

i.   Define the term 'quality management'.

ii. Explain the differences between quality control and quality assurance.

iii. Discuss the difficulties a company may have when trying to achieve quality standards across a global enterprise.

iv. Describe how two technologies could help a company implement quality standards across their global operations.

4. Strategic management

Choose an international company to research. Investigate their website and corporate information. Find the elements of their strategic plan, such as mission statement, values and strategic objectives.

i.   Identify the company, where in the world they operate and list the strategic plan elements you found.

ii. For each element discuss how it may have an impact on the day-to-day operations. How could employees incorporate the values into their work?

iii. Discuss whether the values would translate across cultures or if they may need to be translated or adapted to different countries.

Response

1. Financial ratios

All figures in $000	2016	2015	2014
Revenue			
Domestic	6235	6930	6300
International	520	650	500
Net income	6755	7580	6800
Cost of sales	4700	5000	4200
Gross profit	2055	2580	2600
Operating expenses	1900	2010	1900
Profit (Loss)	155	570	700
Shareholders' equity	4000	4000	4000

Calculate the following profitability ratios for each year:

Ratio	2016	2015	2014
Profit $\frac{\text{Profit}}{\text{Net income}}$			
Gross profit $\frac{\text{Gross profit}}{\text{Net income}}$			
Expenses $\frac{\text{Operating expenses}}{\text{Net income}}$			
Rate of return on equity $\frac{\text{Profit}}{\text{Shareholders' equity}} \times 100$			

Analyse the performance and discuss trends that you have identified.

2. Marketing

You are the marketing manager of a food products company that is considering entering the Indian market. The retail system in India tends to be very fragmented. Also, retailers and wholesalers tend to have exclusive relationships with Indian food companies, which makes access to distribution channels difficult.

i.   What challenges will your company face when entering the market?

ii.   Explain the distribution strategy you would recommend for the company.

3. Financial ratios

Your company is considering the takeover of a small company in an overseas market as a strategy for expansion. The financial stability of the target company is an important factor.

Calculate the current and the debt to equity ratios of the following companies:

Balance sheet items	Target 1	Target 2
Current assets	200 000	100 000
Non-current assets	1 500 000	2 200 000
Total assets	1 700 000	2 300 000
Current liabilities	300 000	400 000
Non-current liabilities	600 000	2 500 000
Total liabilities	900 000	2 900 000
Net assets	800 000	(600 000)
Equity		
Share capital	600 000	200 000
Retained earnings	200 000	(800 000)
Total equity	800 000	(600 000)

Ratio	Target 1	Target 2

Current
  Current assets
  Current liabilities		

Debt to equity
  Total liabilities
  Total equity		

i.   Analyse the ratios.

ii.   Select the best takeover target.

iii. Use the ratios to explain your decision.

4. Environmental scan – Porter's Five Forces

Consider the global market for online training and education. Following are eight aspects of the market. Classify the aspects according to the five forces model.

- Start-up costs are very low.
- Students have access to books, videos, and paper based distance learning packs.
- The more innovative learning sites give lessons for free just for the love of it.
- More people gain access to the web every second.
- Companies, governments and students invest huge amounts in their education.
- There are very few high-quality websites available.
- Traditional colleges and universities are adapting their products for online learning.
- Government legislation in the US and Europe encourages online learning.

Forces	Aspects
New entrants	
Buyer power	
Supplier power	
Substitutes	
Level of competition	

CHAPTER 26
Global leaders and managers

'Management is doing things right,
leadership is doing the right things.'
– Peter Drucker –

MANAGEMENT VERSUS LEADERSHIP

Leaders set the goals and new direction, and challenge the ways things are done. Leaders inspire and motivate people and persuade them to follow their lead. Leaders look into the long term and have a big-picture perspective, understanding the business as a whole.

Managers implement the practical plans to achieve the vision and goals set by leaders. Managers focus on one team, project or department and are set short to medium term goals.

Leaders	Managers
• Leaders develop vision and strategy	• Managers develop policies and procedures
• Leaders inspire and motivate	• Managers direct and control
• Leaders explain why we are doing it	• Managers explain what to do
• Leaders ask questions	• Managers give directions
• Leaders are big-picture oriented	• Managers are bottom-line oriented
• Leadership is doing the right things	• Management is doing things right

Often the two are combined in a job. A manager must set rules, monitor performance and organise resources and at the same time motivate their work team to achieve performance targets and be innovative to solve problems.

Good managers have strong time-management skills; planning and organising time, resources and staff to get the work done. A leader is a visionary and sees the big picture. The work team will benefit from a manager who can support them to do the day-to-day things that will result in the achievement of business goals.

Team development

Bringing people together and putting them in a group does not mean they will automatically operate as an effective team. A model of team development involves four stages as shown here.

Forming

In the first stage of team building, the forming of the team takes place. An individual's behaviour may also be driven by a desire to be accepted by the others and avoid controversy or conflict. Team members are also busy learning about the job, such as organisation of the team, who does what, when to meet and what tasks need to be done. Individuals are gathering information and impressions about each other, about the job and how to approach it.

A leader can help by:

- running inductions and team meetings
- being clear about team goals and responsibilities
- establishing safe work practices
- determining decision-making methods.

Storming

As the team begins to work together, they move into the 'storming' stage. In this stage, the team members compete with each other to exert their authority and for acceptance of their ideas. They have different opinions on what should be done and how it should be done, which causes conflict within the team. Other team members are focused on the tasks and are happy for others to make decisions. As a team progresses through this stage they learn how to work both independently and together as a team. Team members are settling into roles and responsibilities.

The storming stage is necessary to the growth of the team. It can be unpleasant and have an impact on work progress. It will take leadership to guide the group, and resolve conflict so work safety and quality aren't compromised. Tolerance of each team member and their differences needs to be emphasised. Without tolerance and patience the team will fail. This phase can become destructive to the team and will lower motivation if allowed to get out of control.

A leader can help by:

- modelling good teamwork and communication
- solving problems

- enforcing safe work practices and reminding team members about roles and responsibilities
- resolving conflict.

Norming

When the team moves into the 'norming' stage, they are working effectively as a team. They are no longer just focused on themselves but rather are focused on achieving team goals. They respect each other's opinions and value their differences. Working together as a team seems more natural.

In this stage, the team has agreed on ways to get the work done and how they will share information and make decisions. The team members begin to trust each other and actively seek each other out for assistance and feedback. Rather than compete against each other, they are now helping each other to work toward a common goal. The team members also start to make significant progress on the project as they begin working together more effectively. The team manages to have one goal and come to a mutual plan for the team at this stage.

A leader can help by:

- coaching team members
- involving the team in decisions and discussing problems
- recognising good performance
- discussing progress and team goals.

Performing

It is possible for a team to reach a 'performing' stage. This team is able to get the job done smoothly. Team members have become interdependent. By this time they are motivated and experienced.

They can make decisions and problem solve quickly. If there needs to be a change in team processes, the team will come to agreement on changing processes on their own without reliance on the leader.

A leader can help by:

- delegating leadership tasks
- supporting team decisions
- rewarding achievement of team goals
- making sure the team has the tools, equipment and materials they need.

Leadership styles

There are different styles of leadership. A manager will use a style based on their ability and personality, what has worked in the past and what employees respond to best. It is a good idea to understand a range of styles so a manager can adapt their approach according to circumstances, urgency and the people involved. Choosing the best style is based on three factors as shown here.

In this section four leadership styles are examined.

1. Autocratic

The typical autocratic manager does not involve others in the decision-making process. The communication style of an autocratic manager is one-way. They tell staff exactly what they have to do. All decisions are made by the autocratic leader and employees are directed to implement their decisions.

The autocratic style is effective in the workplace where there is a need for urgent action and where the manager is the only one with the experience and expertise. It is common in workplaces that are based on standardised, repetitive processes like a factory or in the kitchens at fast food restaurants. The autocratic manager will focus on making sure staff follow the rules and keep up the pace of production.

2. Behavioural

Douglas McGregor developed his theory X and theory Y in 1960. These opposing perceptions are about how people view work and life in the workplace. McGregor's idea is that the style of a manager will depend on which theory the manager believes to be more true.

X	Y
• People are lazy and will avoid work whenever possible.	• Managers must help employees realise their potential and work towards business goals.
• Managers must control, direct and punish employees to make them work.	• Employees prefer having more control and responsibility over their work life.
• Employees prefer to be told what to do and do not want to take on responsibility.	• People are creative and imaginative and can solve problems.

Theory X will result in a more autocratic approach. Theory Y will result in a more participative style. McGregor recommends managers base their style on theory Y because it will lead to happier, motivated and productive staff.

3. Participative

The participative style is the opposite of the autocratic style and is also called democratic. Employees are involved in the planning and decision making in the workplace. Although the manager may still make the final decision, decisions and plans are based on the ideas and feedback from staff. This style can increase job satisfaction because it gives employees more control over how they work.

This is an effective style where employees are motivated, skilled and experienced. Employees know what to do to get the job done and the role of the manager is to organise resources for the teams and help them solve problems that may arise.

4. Situational

A situational style is one where a manager uses the most appropriate behaviours and adapts their leadership style depending on the situation. Managers adapt their actions, methods of communication and decision making to the situation and are able to utilise multiple styles as conditions change. Managers recognise the strengths and weaknesses of each style and apply this knowledge to a work situation or business challenge.

For example, a manager may prefer a participative style. But the manager knows that the employees in a few branches are inexperienced and will require more direction. In most branches the manager will use a participative style but in the few branches with inexperienced staff a more autocratic approach will be more effective. A manager may use an autocratic style with people working on a production line in a factory but a participative style when planning with factory managers. A manager may use an autocratic approach and then become more participative and situational as the employees become more experienced and increase their expertise over time. A participative manager may also make unilateral decisions now and then when a situation or problem needs urgent attention.

YouTube
Introduction to Business A level: Management styles

Leadership

Leadership is important in a business. Business success depends upon good day-to-day management and a long-term strategic perspective. Leaders help employees and teams define their goals and stay focused on finding ways to achieve them. Leaders use power and persuasion so employees and teams are motivated and understand how they contribute to long-term business success.

By demonstrating the following traits leaders can build a workplace culture and set standards for employee conduct.

Leadership traits that are useful in the workplace include those shown here.

Skilled communicator

Given the challenges of working via interpreters or fumbling through conversations in more than one language, the ability to say clearly what you mean is a key global business skill. Clear communication is a powerful leadership trait to have on the global stage.

Strong communication skills are needed to build business networks, solve problems, negotiate deals and resolve conflict.

Being able to clearly and succinctly describe what you want done is also important. Employees won't all be working towards the same goal if the vision and standards are not clear.

Socially aware

Understanding social and cultural customs and differences is very important when building international business relationships. Recognise that your culture and background are not inherently superior. Adjust eating and sleeping habits to match the local routines and patterns. In other countries, seemingly minor things such as sticking chopsticks in your rice or touching someone with your left hand can be offensive.

Emotional intelligence (EI)

EI is about understanding that people are not always rational and logical but at times affected by emotions. Having EI means that you have empathy and can understand and manage your own emotional reactions to stress, change, events and situations. It also means that you can perceive and work with the emotions of other people and understand how emotions can have an impact on working relationships, teamwork and decisions.

Emotional intelligence is:

- the ability to perceive emotions
- the ability to understand complex emotions
- the ability to regulate emotions to promote better communication and decisions.

Examples of emotional intelligence:

- **Self-awareness:** self-confidence, accurate self-assessment, emotional self-awareness.
- **Social awareness:** empathy, responsiveness to others, organisational awareness.
- **Self-management:** adaptability, emotional self-control, positive outlook, initiative.
- **Relationship management:** conflict management, inspirational leadership, influence, teamwork.

Skilled decision maker

All leaders must make tough decisions. They understand that in certain situations, difficult and timely decisions must be made in the best interests of the entire business; decisions that will not please everyone. Good leaders also know when not to act unilaterally but instead consult others and use collaborative decision making. By being flexible and open-minded to new ideas, the likelihood of the best possible decision is increased.

Future thinker

Having a global perspective and thinking strategically is about using the best people from around the world. To make strategic decisions you need to understand how the business world works on a global scale.

Leaders create a vision and long-term goals for a business and can see how the short-term activities contribute to the long term goals. They keep people motivated by explaining how the day-to-day difficulties and achievements can add up to long-term success.

Leaders also keep scanning the macro business environment and identify threats and opportunities and how to manage them.

Self-disciplined

There is a difference between bosses and workers. Leaders understand the nature of this difference and accept it and how it has an impact on their image, actions and communication. They conduct themselves in a way that sets them apart from their employees. Not in a way that suggests they think they are better than them, but in a way that gives them an objective perspective on everything that's going on in the workplace.

A strong vision and the discipline to see it through is one of the most important characteristics of leadership. The leader who believes in the vision and goals and works toward them will be an inspiration and a resource to their team.

Responsible

Leaders take responsibility for everyone's performance, including their own. They follow up on performance issues, monitor how employees are going and review the effectiveness of company policies and procedures. When things are going well, they praise. When problems arise, they identify them quickly and put solutions in place.

Motivational

The best leaders guide employees through challenges, always on the lookout for solutions to build long-term success. Rather than making things personal when they encounter problems, or blaming individuals, leaders look for constructive solutions and focus on moving forward.

An inspiring leader communicates clearly, concisely and often. By doing so motivates everyone to give their best all the time. They challenge their people by setting high but attainable standards and expectations, and then giving them the support, resources, training and authority to achieve their best. They avoid personal criticism and pessimistic thinking, and look for ways to gain consensus and get people to work together efficiently and effectively as a team.

When things go wrong, employees look to leaders for answers and judge the situation based upon their reaction. If the company is experiencing a major problem, such as a new competitor or economic downturn, it's important to always be confident. A leader's job is to maintain a motivated work environment.

YouTube
What is good leadership? Introverts break it down

CHAPTER 27
Unit 4 People activities

'There is no greater thing you can do with your life
and your work than follow your passions in a
way that serves the world and you'
– Richard Branson –

Topic study

1. List three characteristics of leaders.

2. List three characteristics of managers.

3. Describe the autocratic leadership style.

4. Describe the behavioural leadership style.

5. Explain the difference between McGregor's Theory X and Theory Y.

6. Describe the participative leadership style.

7. Describe the situational leadership style.

8. List three leadership traits.

9. Why does a leader need to be a future thinker?

10. Explain emotional intelligence.

11. You and your partner have got into an argument that has escalated into a shouting match; you're both upset and, in the heat of the anger, making personal attacks you don't really mean. What's the best thing to do? Explain your choice.

    i.   Take a 20-minute break and then continue the discussion.

    ii. Just stop the argument – go silent, no matter what your partner says.

    iii. Say you're sorry and ask your partner to apologise too.

    iv. Stop for a moment, collect your thoughts, then state your case as precisely as you can.

Business research

1. Leadership styles

Different countries tend to develop different approaches to management and corporate culture. People are comfortable with certain leadership styles, some people see managers as friends who are there to encourage and coach while people from other cultures expect a more authoritative approach from a boss.

i.   Consider the following styles; autocratic, participative and situational.

ii.   Discuss each style and the advantages and disadvantages they have in the context of an Australian company operating in a foreign country.

iii. Choose three countries that are trading partners of Australia and discuss which leadership style would best suit the country's culture and how the characteristics of their culture may influence which style would be more suitable.

iv.   Discuss Australian culture and which style is more suitable in domestic businesses.

2. Leadership traits

Research the topic of emotional intelligence (EI).

i.   Define EI and discuss what it is.

ii.   Discuss how EI can help you to manage a diverse workforce.

iii. Discuss how EI can assist you to be a better workplace leader.

3. Leadership styles and traits

This task can be a group task with work assigned and assessed individually. The group will then bring their work together as a group assessed summary presentation.

i.   Explain the team development model of Forming, Storming, Norming and Performing. What is happening at each stage?

ii.   How could an international company, operating with co-workers, suppliers, distributors and customers from different countries affect team development?

iii. For each stage discuss the best leadership style/s to encourage them through to the next stage.

Response

1. Leadership traits

In pairs or small groups develop a code of conduct for leaders of a global company. Develop a list of 10 standards or expectations. Design a slideshow that could be used as an educational tool for managers around the world.

2. Leadership styles

Leadership style questionnaire

Think about what you would do if you were a leader in a global business. Out of the options given choose the one you think you are more likely to do.

1. Your work team is having trouble getting started. You have tried to make everyone feel comfortable. You have allowed time to get acquainted. Everyone seems interested and cooperative, but reluctant to speak up.

    a. Wait until they're ready to speak up.
    b. Suggest that the group vote on what to do next.
    c. Allocate some specific assignments to different people and help them complete their assignments.

2. The team is operating extremely well. Members get along well with each other. Discussion is lively. Everyone is contributing to the work. You want to make sure this continues.

    a. Reduce your leadership. Let group members lead the group as much as possible.
    b. Be sure agreement is reached on each point before proceeding.
    c. Keep the group firmly under your control or the group will lose its momentum.

3. The team has been very productive. Two or three members have done most of the work. Everyone seems happy, but you would like to make some changes so that more members will get involved.

    a. Tell it like it is. Outline the changes and see that they are made.
    b. Propose the changes. Explain why they are needed, then let the group decide what will be done.
    c. Don't do anything that might threaten group productivity.

4. The team is working well and team members are working well together. You feel somewhat unsure about your lack of direction of the team.

    a. Leave the group alone.
    b. Slowly assert yourself to give the group more direction.
    c. Ask the group if you should provide more direction, then comply with their wishes.

5. The team was going great, but now it is falling apart. Members are beginning to argue. It is hard to stay focused on the work and there is conflict amongst team members.

    a. Let everyone have their say. Don't get involved.
    b. Take a vote on what to do.
    c. Propose a review of the jobs and goals for the team. If no one strongly disagrees, reassign jobs and clarify team goals.

6. Your group has completed a project to a high standard but now no one seems to know what to do and how to take the next step.

    a. Suggest that the group move on to another project. If no one disagrees, list possible projects.

    b. Choose a project for the team and assign jobs.

    c. Just keep quiet until the team works it out for themselves.

SCORING YOUR LEADERSHIP STYLE TENDENCIES

Each of the three possible solutions corresponds to one of the three styles of leadership:

Problem	Autocratic	Participative	Situational
1	C	B	A
2	C	B	A
3	A	B	C
4	B	C	A
5	C	B	A
6	B	A	C

Assess your results and your leadership style preferences

*   In problem I, the team needs direction. Voting would not be useful. A non-directive approach might work in the long run, but would be frustrating in the short term. (c) is the best solution.

*   In problem 2, there is no problem. 'If it isn't broke, don't fix it!' (a) is the best solution.

*   In 3, the team is productive, but not everyone is contributing. The team needs help but a directive approach (a) might cause a rebellion. A non-directive (c) style would not get the quiet members involved. Go with (b).

*   Problem 4 is similar to 2. The team is working well. Resist the temptation to take action when none is needed. Try (a).

*   In problem 5, the team was all right, but now it is not. Leadership is required. Non-directive (a) leadership will only worsen the situation. If you vote (b), frustration may get in the way of reason. Directive leadership (c) is the best bet.

*   In 6, democratic leadership (a) is called for. A directive (b) approach would oppose the team's stated position. Since the team is at a stalemate, solution (c), the non-directive style, would not help.

CHAPTER 28
Unit Four
Examination questions

'In all of our actions, we must seek to be living examples of the
change we wish to see in the world, by walking the path,
we make the path visible.'

– Phil Lane Jr –

The structure of the examination for Year 12 ATAR Business Management and Enterprise is:

Section	Number of questions	Number that must be answered	Marks per question	Suggested working time in minutes	Total marks
1: Short Answer	6	6	10	100	60
2: Extended Answer	3	2	20	80	40
				Total	100

This chapter contains short answer and extended answer questions that reflect the content in Unit 4 of the Year 12 ATAR course. Students can use these questions to prepare for the ATAR exam.

Questions from this chapter can also be used to construct an examination for school based assessment.

Short answer questions

Question 1

i. What are three ways we can understand culture? (2 marks)

ii. Explain how understanding of customs and etiquette can help with developing global business. (2 marks)

iii. How can a country's education levels affect global business? (2 marks)

iv. What is corporate social responsibility (CSR)? What three advantages can it offer a global company? (4 marks)

Question 2

i.   What is inflation? What causes inflation? (2 marks)

ii. Discuss how interest rates can have an impact on business if they are falling and rising.
     (4 marks)

iii. Explain the economic impact of a rising Australian dollar and a falling Australian dollar. (4 marks)

Question 3

i.   Describe a source of internal funding. (2 marks)

ii. Describe three sources of external funding a company could access to fund global expansion. (6 marks)

iii. List two types of financial institutions. (2 marks)

Question 4

i.   Discuss how political factors can affect global business. (3 marks)

ii. Legal factors also have an impact on business. What is a patent? Discuss how patent registration can be used in global business. (3 marks)

iii. What is e-commerce? Identify three ways it can be used to expand into international markets. (3 marks)

Question 5

i.   What is the purpose of a strategic plan? (2 marks)

ii. List three tools that can be used to conduct an environmental scan. Explain how one works. (5 marks)

iii. What are three examples of strategic goals that can drive business strategy. (3 marks)

Question 6

i.   Define and interpret the ratio below. How can it be improved? (4 marks)

Expenses	$\dfrac{\text{Operating costs}}{\text{Net income}}$	$\dfrac{160\,000}{720\,000}$	$= 0.22$

ii. Define and interpret the ratio below. How can it be improved? (4 marks)

Debt to equity	$\dfrac{\text{Total liabilities}}{\text{Closing equity}}$	$\dfrac{325\,000}{195\,000}$	$= 1.67$

iii. Outline two limitations of using ratio analysis. (2 marks)

Question 7

i.   Product development involves innovation. Outline the difference between incremental and disruptive innovation. Include an example of each. (4 marks)

ii. What are three things that are considered when product ideas are evaluated? (3 marks)

iii. Why is intellectual property protection important for product development? Identify two forms of protection a company could use. (3 marks)

Question 8

i. What are the three aspects quality management is based on? (3 marks)

ii. Why is feedback important for quality control? (2 marks)

iii. Discuss the differences between Just in time and Just in case inventory management. List three factors to consider when deciding which method to use. (5 marks)

Question 9

i. What are three ways leaders are different to managers? (3 marks)

ii. Discuss the difference between an autocratic style and a participative style of management. Include an example of when each style is best. (4 marks)

iii. What is the situational management style? Discuss a situation where the style is the best approach. (3 marks)

Extended answer questions

Question 1

A company's mission statement should have a global focus. A company must have a clear set of objectives to develop long-term plans to focus on global markets. Global strategic planning aims to develop an effective global strategy. Part of the process is to evaluate the internal and external environments and make decisions about how to achieve long-term objectives.

i. Discuss the purpose of strategic planning. Outline a tool a company could use to conduct an environmental scan as part of strategic planning and how it works. (5 marks)

ii. Explain the role of the following technologies on business expansion into global markets:
   – online payment systems
   – social media
   – digital distribution of products   (7 marks)

iii. Discuss two of the following four factors that affect global operations. Provide examples for each factor.
   – economic activity
   – cultural considerations
   – political
   – legal systems   (8 marks)

Question 2

Asia is a collection of nations in various stages of development. Nations have different political and social structures, cultures, economic conditions, legal environments and consumer preferences.

The Asia Pacific region offers growth opportunities for Australian companies. The region has become important to growth for the Australian economy and presents some of the best opportunities for companies worldwide.

i. Discuss two technologies and how they could assist an Australian company to enter Asian markets. (6 marks)

ii. Discuss four cultural considerations that could make Asian expansion challenging. (8 marks)

iii. Outline two strategic alliances that an Australian business could use to enter markets in Asia. Explain which one you would recommend. (6 marks)

Question 3

You are considering a takeover of a target company in the Asia Pacific region. There are government approvals to get but you are evaluating financial data to make a final decision.

Ratios	Last year	This year
Gross profit	49c	47c
Profit	31c	24c
Expenses	18c	22c
Debt to equity	$0.70	$1.20

i. Discuss an ethical issue that may arise when working with foreign government officials. (3 marks)

ii. Interpret the ratios. What does each ratio mean and what do the results show? (12 marks)

iii. Discuss your analysis and make a recommendation. What could your company do to improve the ratios? (5 marks)

Question 4

Global leaders need to understand the factors that shape international business relationships by examining cultural differences. Managers working outside their domestic environments can find their companies' norms are inconsistent with businesses in the foreign market.

> 'I learned early in my career that my business leadership style was to influence and build effective teams. And so I've had to try to change that a little bit – at the same time, change my teams to be more independent and responsible for decisions on their own.'
>
> Diane Jurgens, General Motors

i. Describe the characteristics of each of the following leadership styles:
   – autocratic
   – participative
   – situational (9 marks)

ii. How could cultural characteristics of a country influence which leadership style is more effective? (5 marks)

iii. Discuss how the following traits would help a manager successfully work with global partners:
   – skilled communicator
   – socially aware
   – future thinker (6 marks)